The Author Prof. Dr. B.B. Puri, Senior Architect who has written more than 100 books. His books have been released by president of India at Rashtrapati Bhawan & other V.V.I.P's he has been decorated with many National & International Awards.

This book is recommended specially for Architects, Interior Designer, Builders, Contractor and persons connected with Building Industries.

Many Architects has recommended this book as text book in the colleges of Architects & Interior Designers.

Add Color in Your Life

Through

Vastu Shastra: A Science of Vedic Architecture

Prof. Dr. B.B. Puri

Books For All

Delhi

Vastu Research Centre (VRC)
Research Institute of Vedic Culture (Regd. Charitable Trust, NGO)
Registered Office:
W–151, Greater Kailash I
New Delhi-110048

First Published 2017

ISBN 978-81-7386-320-2
ISBN 81-7386-320-2

Published by
Books For All
(an imprint of Low Price Publications)
A-6, 2nd Floor, Nimri Commercial Centre,
Near Ashok Vihar Phase-IV, Delhi-110052
Phones: 011-27302453
e-mail: info@Lppindia.com
Website: www.Lppindia.com

Printed at
D K Fine Art Press P Ltd.
Delhi-110052

PRINTED IN INDIA

Contents

Foreword

Er. Suresh Kumar Puri
Director General (Road Development)
& Special Secretary (Retd.)
Ministry of Road Transport & Highways
Govt. of India
B-221, Sushant Lok – 1
Gurgaon, Haryana – 122 002

After the successful launch and a good reception by the readers to Dr. B. B. Puri's books on the subject of "Vedic Architecture and Art of Living", "Vastu Science for 21st Century 'to enjoy the gift of Nature", "Applied Vastu Shastra in Modern Architecture", " Mass Scale Housing for Hot climate", among others, I am deeply humbled and honoured to be asked to write a foreword for his latest book titled **"Add Color in Your Life, through Vastu Shastra, A Science of Vedic Architecture".**

Having known Prof. Dr. B.B. Puri since last few decades and beingan ardent admirer of his works, I am glad to note that he has continued with his quest to establish a connection between the ancient Indian cultures, the architecture, interior designing and the environment, with an ultimate aim to achieve peaceful living for the mankind, which is quite evident in his latest book as well.

Considering that the modern Architecture tends to ape the West in creating closed box like structures with an artificial environment, it is exciting to learn about the possibility of healthy, peaceful living with nature, through the knowledge of Vastu Shastra, the Science of Vedic Architecture. Prof. Dr. B.B. Puri, in this book has explained at length about the Vedantic thoughts, Architecture programming, in the context of Vedic tradition on Hindu Architecture.

The Vastu principles were formulated, keeping in view, the cosmic influence of the sun, its light & heat, solar energy, the air pressure and the direction of the wind, the earth's magnetic field, the orientation of the site and the influence of the cosmic energies on our planet earth. There is a general awareness to the principles of Vastu Science and the growing desire that these principles are taken into consideration while planning and building their homes and other structures.

Prof. Puri's attempt to highlight the principles of Vastu Science & its applications in designing of modern built environment is commendable. It is worthwhile for the architects, contractors, interior designers, builders to equip themselves with this ancient yet valuable knowledge.

The books written by Prof. Dr. B.B. Puri provide for an excellent background for developing a curriculum to encourage other scholars of Vastu Science to record their knowledge and enrich this field for the future generations.

Prof. Puri's attempt to continue to author books on Vastu Science & his efforts in spreading the knowledge of Vastu Shastra is truly remarkable.

S.K Puri

Council of Architecture
(Incorporated under the Architects Act, 1972)

J R Bhalla
New President

5 Sunder Nagar
New Delhi- 110003
Phone : 4618252, 461823
Fax : 011-4618252

26th July, 1995

Foreword

It gives me great pleasure to write this foreword to Prof. B.B. Puri's work on Vedic Architecture and Art of Living. Prof. Puri has done a deep study into the relationship between the ancient Indian culture, the architecture, the environment and the resultant recipe for peaceful living. He has drawn extensively from the Vedas, Upanishad and the Gita.

Considering the modern Architectural trends to ape the West in producing closed box like structures with artificial environment, it is refreshing to know about the Art of Living in peace with nature. To that extent Prof. Puri has done a single service in bringing about the present work.

Prof. Puri in his book has discussed Vedantic thoughts, architectural programming in the context of Vedic traditions, the mandala, drawing heavily on Hindu Architects.

I commend this book not only to the student of architecture but others in practice who whilst finalising their concept should draw inspiration from our well established and tested principles enshrined in Vedic culture. His advice to young architects and student as such is timely and deserves consideration.

8B, Shankar Market, Connaught Circus, New Delhi-110001,

Phone/Fax: 3325027

Foreword

Vastu Science for 21st Century is the latest contribution by the author, Prof. B.B. Puri, after an overwhelming response to his earlier books tilted Vedic Architecture and Art of Living, Applied Vastu Shastra in Modern Architecture and Vastu Shastra for Mass Housing. Vastu Shastra is not merely an art but a definite science in itself. This book has made an excellent effort to establish this fact. The knowledge of Vastu is based on Vedic literature and is derived from the fundamental principles of Vedantic knowledge.

Prof. B.B. Puri is a well-known architect, having a vast experience in the field of architecture. He is the founder of Vastu Kala Academy, the School of Architecture and Interior Designing. He is also the founder of Vastu Research Centre. He has brought out in clear terms that the knowledge of modern architecture is incomplete without Vastu Science. The Vastu principles have been formulated keeping in view the cosmic influences of the sun, the direction of the wind, the position of moon, the earth's magnetic field and the influence of the entire cosmos on our planet.

Prof. Puri's attempt to highlight the principles of Vastu Science and its application in designing of built environment is commendable. It is highly desirable that all our young architects are equipped with this knowledge and they make use of it in their day-to-day design activities. To achieve this objective, it would be necessary to incorporate the knowledge of Vastu science in the curricula of Architecture, Town

Planning and Engineering Colleges and Universities. The series of books written by Prof. Puri provide an excellent background for developing such a curriculum and encourage other scholars of Vastu to record their experience and knowledge in this field.

I pray the almighty to bless Prof. B.B. Puri to continue his efforts in spreading the knowledge of Vastu science.

Dr. P.S. Rana

Chairman & M.D. HUDCO

Roda Mistry,
Plot No. 257, Road No. 18,
Jubilee Hills, Co-op. Housing Society,
Jubilee Hills,
Hyderabad-500034

Introduction

The author's deep knowledge of Vedic Period Architecture is clearly seen from the different chapters of the book especially Chapter VIII 'Global Study of Architecture in Vedic Period', where will make contents of this book very interesting for the reader.

Dr. B.B. Puri is known to be a very creative man not just in the field of Architecture but in all aspects connected with it especially the mind of the person who wishes to indulge in the process of construction in India and his dedication of the book Vedic Architecture to 'Lord Krishna' gives it a touch of the mystic.

We wish him success in this and all other future endeavors.

Smt. Roda Mistry

Former M.P. (1980-1986)

Acknowledgement

I wish to express my heartfelt thanks to all my readers for their wholehearted encouragement and support for my previous books on the some subject. Their appreciation and unstinted encouragement has gone a long way in inspiring me to write this book.

A special tribute to Late Mr. Harbans Grover Sr. Architect, New York, USA my Ex. Partner, for always giving me encouragement & guidance.

I would like to thank Mr. S.K Puri for writing a very detailed forward for this book.

My thanks to Mr. J.R. Bhalla, & Dr. P.S. Rana for book review.

I wish to give my blessings to the noble soul Miss Aarti Kanojia for taking special interest & pain in composition of the manuscript and conceptualizing the computerized diagrams and front Jacket design of this book.

I offer my sincere regards to readers, all my clients who have faith in Vastu science, Ph.d. Students, Staff, Faculty of Vastu Research Centre, Design Gurukul and Building Doctors, Grover & Puri Architect Since 1960, and all members of Research Institute of Vedic Culture and Association of Scientific Vastu Experts.

B.B. PURI

Author

1

The Rudiments of Vedantic Thoughts

Preamble

It is a misconception that 'nature' is hostile to man. If approached in true harmony, its secrets can be revealed and the energies harnessed for the benefit of the living beings. But any relation of competition and conquest is not only productive but ultimately leads to environment and ecological disparities, which is 'unnatural'.

The ancient philosophic concept represents two different logical processes-the inductive and deductive. The former took its stand upon 'Smriti' or reasoned knowledge and the law of cause and effect and the latter depended upon insight or inspiration, known as 'Shruti' or divine revelation, of which the Vedas are said to be the highest expression. In the modern language, we may call these as objective or atheistic science and subjective or theistic science towards the finer and more subtle aspects of life and consciousness.

The specialist approach of the objective sciences has developed during the last three hundred years of the scientific and industrial revolution and the post-war (1945) management and information developments. The scope of research is strictly within the physical phenomena. (Incidentally, one finds these developments in the cold regions of the world where absolute physical survival is of critical priority for like sustains and manifest. Nature is hostile to man and the man-nature relations are of competition and conquest.)

In the holistic approach, the physical and metaphysical, theistic and atheistic man, environment, objectives, mediums, tools are all considered as inseparable whole, because each is a part of, and a cause of, the evolutionary process of this great act of cosmic creative cycle. Here too, one finds clear scope and 'thresholds' of specialised fields, but, at all the scales, the central theme is holistic, and one is constantly reminded of being 'the part within the part, the whole around the whole, the universe within the universe' concept. The contexts of CONSCIOUSNESS, LIFE and MAN are complementary, constant and central. This is also called 'subtropical science'. (One finds this culture develop around the tropical and sub-tropical river valleys, where physical survival was not critical due to friendly eco-cultural relationships. Evolution of Mind and Spirit take natural priority. The 'physical' does not pose apparent limitations for life and living. It only remains an essential base from where one takes off the journey towards the finer and more subtle aspects of life and consciousness.)

These are various thought processes. There was further development into Puranas. Arts, science and technologies also developed to highly refined levels. Mathematics, astronomy astrology, arts, literature, music, dance, sculpture, painting, ,medicine, metallurgy, etc. also developed to similar levels. (Interestingly, development of long span structures did not catch attention, probably because the local weather did not need these.) Hindu, Jaina and Buddhist are three major processes of architecture and town planning in India among the Vedic creations.

I started to write this book because I needed it myself. I was also keen to find answer to the question as to why the ancient architecture suddenly became so attractive to the Western world. This compilation is a humble attempt to discover Vedic Architecture synchronizing with the Art of Living. The present-day life of the people about to enter the twenty 1st century is so complicated, illogical and contradictory that any attempt to describe a period fully would fill reams of paper. I have attempted to take a microscopic section from the magnificent Vedic period based on 'Truth' and scientific reason to show how much the people are close to nature and they should learn the art of meaningful and fruitful living aided by architectural role, by giving importance of color in their life.

I am aware of the difficulties and limitations set in the path of any enterprise to seek learning form the Vedas and the Upanishads. Such a venture, despite my best efforts, cannot be claimed to be a comprehensive study of such a vast ocean of knowledge. Our aim has to be the discovery of 'Truth', and in order to attain this goal, we must apply our minds fearlessly and without prejudice or preconception and formulate our conclusion on the basis of available evidence as far as they permit us to do so. To achieve the desired benefit in true spirit, great care is to be taken to distinguish clearly the 'Known' from the 'Unknown' and to approach the. 'Un-manifest' from 'Manifest'.

Architecture regulates the relation between man and his environments. An architect should exhibit his skills by overcoming the difficulties and differences between the principles laid down in the 'Vedas' and the need of the present-day requirements, keeping in mind the original relation between man and nature and to find acceptable solutions. For good results, it is more important to put correct questions than to find answers to wrong questions.

We have to bring into harmony the common values, moral codes, individual beliefs, ideological convictions, economic conditions, social obligations and cultural symbolisations, coupled with philosophical ideas and meaningful environment. In the Vedic period, people built homes, temples and hermitages not merely to be used as shelter but mainly with a view to have a peaceful place for offering prayers and to pursue peace and to live in common harmony. But, in the modern world, people built concrete clusters mainly for a high rate of return. After the Second World War, the architectural practice just turned out to be a race towards the so-called modernisation, adopting bureaucratic values, resulting in world-wide pollution, environmental and ecological problems, with no peace of mind under any kind of shelter.

The ancient philosophic concept represents two different logical processes- the 'Inductive' and 'Deductive'. The former took its stand upon 'Smriti' or reasoned knowledge and the law of cause and effect and the latter depended upon insight or inspiration, known as 'Shruti' or divine revelation, of which the Vedas are said to be the highest expression. In the modern language, we may call these as an objective or atheistic science and subjective or theistic science towards the finer and more subtle aspects of life and consciousness.

One ponders to find answers to vital questions like: what was the beginning? How did the universe evolve? What is the real constitution of a human being? What is the ultimate? etc. the Vedas proclaim that Consciousness, the Universal Will, the Omnipresent and the Omnipotent 'Brahman' (Purusha) is without beginning or end. The 'Eternal' contains Space (Akash), Time (Kala), Energy (Pran) and Nature (Prakriti). The all-pervading consciousness regulates the entire cosmos and illumines or gives spark of life to all individual beings. Death and decay are the Vedas propound that aside from the physical body, an individual constitutes his mind and his intellect and is presided over or enlivened by the cosmos consciousness. The mind functions two-folds—to acquire knowledge though the five senses (Gyanindrias) and to act in the world outside through the five related organs (Karam-indrias). The five basic elements of nature, namely, the space, air, fire, water and earth, correspond to sensations of hearing, touch, sight, taste and smell, respectively. Intellect is the discriminating power in us, to take decisions for elevation to righteousness or to indulge in sensual short-lived pleasures; to Endeavour to rediscover alpha and omega of the Reality or to succumb to desires and remain in worldly illusions.

Our existence comprises three states of awareness, namely, waking, dream and deep-sleep stages. Also we have three behavioral qualities, 'Satvic', 'Rajas' and 'Tamas'; that is, spiritual, psychological or merely phusical ways of living. We are taught that by knowledge, by selfless service and by meditation, we can achieve the Ultimate. Knowledge can be derived from 'Yantras', creativity from 'Tantras', energies from 'Mantras' and inspiration from 'Meditation', the secret laws of nature.

Despite materialistic development, resources and reaches, the westerners are looking to the Orient for desired peace of mind. India is the source, the fountain-head of the vast ancient Vedic knowledge available on the planet today. This open secret is relatively unknown. When the Vedic concept is presented through modern technological advances, the sublime information becomes available for all walks of life and be easily understood. This would give a new outlook in the world of architecture, art and science.

In my fifty five years of professional experience as an architect, Vastu Consultant & Author I have had many opportunities in India and abroad to study and deal with people having different cultures and style of living and varied problems facing them, which I have endeavored to discuss in this book. I have also kept in view the demands made at the International Conferences by the Western people to know more about the Indian philosophy, with particular reference to the Vedic architecture, which inspired me to start writing. In August 1990, I had the honor of delivering lectures on this subject at the invitation of the international organization 'Moscow project Management Institution'. Russian high light our Indian culture.

During my studies and profession, I have always been keenly interested in ancestral culture and habitat, particularly during the most ancient 'Vedic' period. This entailed a lot of research, as there is no readily available history of Vedic architecture. It has been fascinating to dig out and find that the living of our ancestors was really scientific.

For the purpose of the reckoning of the Vedic Age, no definite period has been envisaged in this book. The rise of the Vedic knowledge in architecture and its subsequent application in later periods in the Indian history of architecture has been taken into account. The author does not wish to go into the controversy of the exact period of the Vedic Age.

'Sanskrit' quotation –

"Na pranena na apranena martyo jivati kaschana,
Itarena tu jivanti yasmin etavapasritau."

Meaning:

Our life does not depend merely on the breathing process. The intake of diet is indeed important for health, but health does not rest on food alone, because everything can be thrown out of order if the mind is upset. A turbulence injected into the mind is enough to disturb the entire balance of personality. Your strength is in you. Religion begins where science ends—the beginning of higher wisdom.

Accomplishment of an architect includes development of relationship between the "situation", namely, surroundings, climate, land form, view, topography, light and its manifestations, color, reflections, etc., and the "medium", namely, materials and construction techniques. Design is a learning process. Man, surroundings and methods are integral to each other and, therefore, any design action is relative and requires holistic, meditative and creative processes. Similarly, nature, man and product are within evolutionary network guided by performance standards. Architecture is to be seen, felt, perceived, conceived and experienced from inside as well as outside. It has to have fourth dimension.

The Universe is governed by the positive laws with innumerable names and forms, constantly changing, moving and transforming. Ever fresh, even death and destruction are the source of new creations:

Time, movements, transformations, information's, thoughts, creation, destruction exist ever since. LIKE DESIGN EXISTS EVER SINCE.

The Mind is the unique creation of the Great Designer. To enjoy this grand play of consciousness, the Leela of Purusha and Prakriti, one has to observe it discover it, create out of it and merge into it again. The "Adwaitas" call this a singular play of consciousness. The "Dwaitas" call this the dance grandouts between the Mind and Consciousness. This is the game of Creation.

MIND is the author and the lord of man's physical world around.

Evolution

One ponders to find answers to vital questions like:

What was the beginning of the beginning? (PURUSHA)-Man

How did all these evolve? (PRAKRITI)-Nature

How can one say relevant form irrelevant?

What is the ultimate?

There are many questions the 'atheists' and the 'rationalists' are equally interested. Both have theories. And, the important ones are also parallel. But many questions remain unanswered. Also, the paradox is that the more one is informed, the less he knows!

If there was 'nothing' before the beginning, how did anything begin? (A big theory)

This is a humble attempt in giving a glimpse of habitation and the way of life in the ancient India. As far as possible, my submissions on the inter-relationship of architecture vis-a-vis art of living in unison with the nature as expounded in the Vedic age are supported by diagrams, charts, illustrations and photographs.

The views expressed in this book are strictly personal and do not reflect any body's opinion.

2

History of Vedic Vastu Architecture

Foundation of Indian Civilization and Vedic Vastu Philosophy

The aim of the Vedic Vastu philosophy was to discover first, the secret laws of the universe and then from them to shape a pattern of every-day life. The Indo-Aryan village was, therefore, conceived of as a universe in itself on a small scale. The five social grades, partly based upon race and partly upon occupation, were the four recognized Varnas, known as the 'pure classes'–the Brahmins, the Kshatriyas, the Vaishyas and the Shudras and the fifth class comprising the offspring of inter-marriages not recognized by the Aryan law. These 'five people of the Aryan community represented the five elements of the universe, and each had a part of the village assigned to it, symbolising a small division of that universe.

The Brahmins (Priests) acquired the most prominent place among the five peoples or 'Panch-Jana'. At birth, the Brahmin stood on a level common to the Kshatriya, Vaishya and Shudra. It was only at the ceremony of investiture with the sacred thread and initiation into the state of Brahmacharya or studentship, when his spiritual father, the Brahmin guru, whispered in his ear the mystic formula, the Gayatri Mantra, which contained the essence of all the Vedas, that he was born to Brahminhood.

The Kshatriyas formed the Aryan fighting clans. Their specific duty was the protection of the whole community and the administration of justice. Though they were the ruling community, they were ranked lower than the Brahmins – the spiritual leaders of the people.

The Vaishya class, which included agriculturists, traders and craftsmen, was not bound by such strict rules of morality as the two upper classes, since trafficking and usury were 'satyanrita' or mixture of truth and falsehood. Yet, the ancient code of Aryan ethics declares that "of all pure things, purity within in acquiring wealth is pronounced the most excellent. Since he who gains wealth with clean hands is truly pure. Even in Vedic times, the trading community was an influential one among the Aryans in India.

Shudras were the lowest of the four classes not recognized as 'pure' as Aryans. They were not permitted to wear the sacred thread, the symbol of a second or spiritual birth, and their highest duty, according to 'manu', was the service of the Brahmins with the expectation that if faithfully performed, it might win for them Brahminhood in the next birth.

Outside the four Varnas, but still included within the Aryan pale was a fifth class called Samanya or common alias Sutas, which was formed by irregular inter-marriages between the other classes or between the Aryans and the non-Aryans.

Every member of the Brahmin, Kshatriya and Vaishya family, wearing the sacred thread or 'Yajnopavita' was supposed to perform religious duties. "The morning Sandhya includes various practices- bathing in the running water, breathing exercises, and recitation of the Gakyatri, the most sacred of all formulae (Mantras)."

'Sanskrit' shloka –

"Om bhur bhuvah svah Tat Savitur Varenyam

Bhargo devasya dhimahi Dhiyo yo nah prachodayat."

Meaning:

(The first line contains Om, the mighty monosyllable, the Alpha and Omega of all reality, followed by the names of the three octosyllabic lines from the Rigveda: "That desirable glory of the God Savitur, may we possess it. It will awaken our thoughts"), and other Vedic text. Then five "great sacrifices" (Mahayajna) – offering to the Gods (deva), demons (bhuta), and ghosts of the dead (pitri), to men (nri) by the exercise of hospitality, and to the Brahmin by the reading of a Vedic test. 'After that honour is paid to the five idols of the home (ayatana) symbolizing Vishnu, Shiva, Durga, Ganesha, and Surya, morning and evening there is an agnihotra, a sacrifice of fire.

The Sandhya, or daily ritual of the Brahmin, performed at sunrise, noon, and sunset, also belongs to the immemorial traditions of the Aryan religion, in which the sun was worshipped as the symbol of the unknown power in the universe, governing all other natural powers.

This tradition grew up with the organization of the Aryan village, in which Managalavithi, i.e., a path surrounding the village, was consecrated for the performance of the rite of 'Pradakshina' symolising the path of the sun across the heavens or the turning of the wheel of life and death. (COSMIC CROSS – refer to Diag. No.1)

The sites of the villages were carefully chosen according to principles. Firstly, ritualistic – governed by the Indo-Aryan rites as discussed earlier, and, secondly, sanitary, as expounded in the Shilpa Shastras and observed in the traditions of the Indo-Aryan master builder. The villages were generally situated on the river banks, by the sea shore or by the side of a lake, not only because of the requirement of the agrarian Aryan community but because of the ample bathing facilities provided by them. Bathing was regarded as a religious rite in itself, and a necessary preliminary for sacrificial

rites. A flowing stream was always preferred to the stagnant one out of sanitary considerations. The 'Devas' or the 'Shining ones', who were the guardian spirits of the Aryan people, loved the places which by nature or by careful planning, were provided with water and pleasant gardens.

The Aryan way of life gave rise of the symbolism which also became an inseparable aspect of the Indo-Aryan villages. We find the philosophy of an individual mingled with his total environment. Such a unique inter-relation of a man and his town is not to be found anywhere in the world. The expounders of the Shilpa Shastras had done a commendable job in moulding the religious philosophy in the physical forms of the village planning. The typical form, probably derived from the fortified camp of the early Aryans, was a rectangular enclosure with its four sides facing the four quarters, divided into four wards by the two main streets, which crossed each other in the centre and terminated at the four ends by four principal gates. There were four subsidiary gates near the corners of the village enclosure so that the whole circumference of the walls was divided into eight – 'the eight-fold path'. (Refer to Diag. No. 2A & 2B)

The Kautiliya Arthshastra, one of the oldest treatises on politics and sociology, gives the names of the four principal gates of the Aryan town or village. The eastern gate, the starting point of the circumcubulatory rite, was dedicated to Brahma, the Creator, represented by the rising sun. The southern gate, which symbolised the sun at noon, was dedicated to Indra, the Vedic God, who ruled the firmament during the day. The western gate was dedicated to the setting sun, or to Yama, the Lord of Death, and the northern gate to Senapati or Kartikeya, the War God. The nature of symbolism of the Vedas was changed into the philosophic concept of the Upanishads. Vishnu- Surya took the place of Indra at the Zenith, Siva was substituted for Yama and Vishnu-Narayana replaced Kartikeya. It was on this symbolic rite of Indo-Aryan village-the rite of wheel of life – that the Buddha based his doctrine of eight-fold path.

The Vedic religion was, thus, the moving spirit of the organization of the Aryan village communities. The Indian lore is full of laws given in crystallized form by saints and scholars in every branch of learning. The process by which such universal laws were arrived at may be unknown to us, but these formulae, in most cases, are found perfect and are applicable even today. Nothing was left undirected. The execution of even the minutest detail had laws governing it.

The principles laid down for the construction of dwellings, even today, seem amazingly scientific. The religious mystery given to the whole process gave birth to superstitions that generally arise from exaggerating a logical reasoning. The religious connotation was probably employed to keep the law makers (kings) and the Brahmins (priests) from being transparent. Rituals gave the whole process a sacred dimension, which saw to it that every little detail was efficiently carried out.

Dwelling

While creating dwelling, the basic idea was always to recreate symbolically a universe. It was intended to adequately circumscribe a consecrated piece of ground or which to maintain, during the sojourn on earth, a living contact with the transcendental principle. The concept of a house, however, has been changing over the times. In the Rig Vedic period, a house was looked upon as a temple. Later (1500 BC), it was compared to a womb (as a child grows secure in a mother's womb: man prayed for similar security and peace).

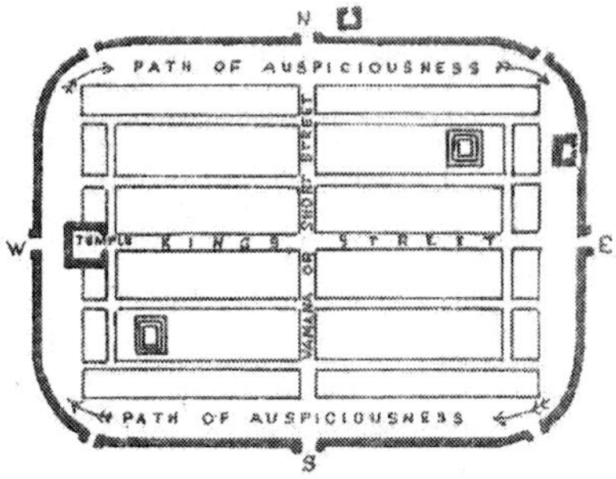

Ashrama or Hermitage for Brahmin

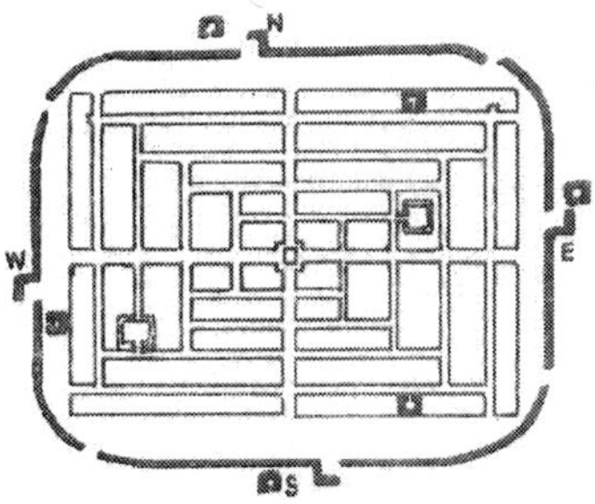

For a mixed population including all the four Varnas.
(Corrected for Ram Raj Architecture of Hindus)

INDO-ARYAN VILLAGE PLAN

Diag. 2A

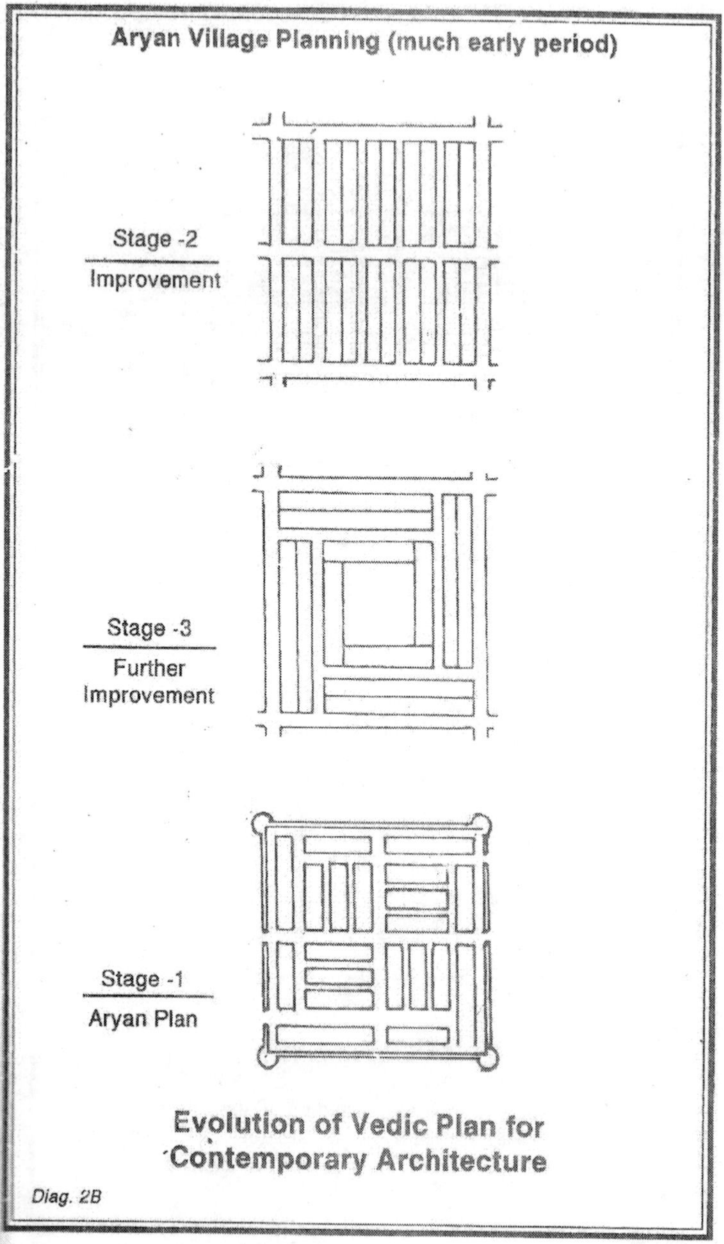

Harrapan City at Lothal Remains from From 2200 B.C.

Recent excavation at Lothal located 87 km southwest of Ahmedabad in Gujarat has proved that it was one of the important cities of the 5,000 years old Indus Valley civilization. The Lothal remains show a settlement of the pre-Aryan Harappan era, dating as far back as 2200 B.C.Lothal adds a new chapter to the history of India by extending the geographical limits of the contemporary Egyptian and Sumerian societies. The find is of tremendous significance for its invaluable archaeological evidences. Especially, it bears the testimony of great engineering and technical achievements of people. Excavation at, Lothal has unearthed a well-planned port city with an elaborate system of drainage, wells houses with arrangements for baths and fireplaces. In order to protect city form frequent floods, a large mud-brick wall was constructed enclosing the citadel or acropolis and the lower town of Lothal. The houses were made up of sun-dried brick which ranged in size from 28 * 12.8* 6.3 to35.6* 18*8.9 cm. In drains and baths lime mortar was used as binding material. The floor was lime plastered. One important building of Lothal was the warehouse measuring 40m * 50 m built on a four-metre high podium of bricks.

Recent excavation at Lothal located 87 km southwest of Ahmedabad in Gujarat has proved that it was one of the important cities of the 5,000 years old Indus Valley civilization. The Lothal remains show a settlement of the pre-Aryan Harappan era, dating as far back as 2200 B.C.Lothal adds a new chapter to the history of India by extending the geographical limits of the contemporary Egyptian and Sumerian societies. The find is of tremendous significance for its invaluable archaeological evidences. Especially, it bears the testimony of great engineering and technical achievements of people. Excavation at, Lothal has unearthed a well-planned port city with an elaborate system of drainage, wells houses with arrangements for baths and fireplaces. In order to protect city form frequent floods, a large mud-brick wall was constructed enclosing the citadel or acropolis and the lower town of Lothal. The houses were made up of sun-dried brick which ranged in size from 28 * 12.8* 6.3 to35.6* 18*8.9 cm. In drains and baths lime mortar was used as binding material. The floor was lime plastered. One important building of Lothal was the warehouse measuring 40m * 50 m built on a four-metre high podium of bricks.

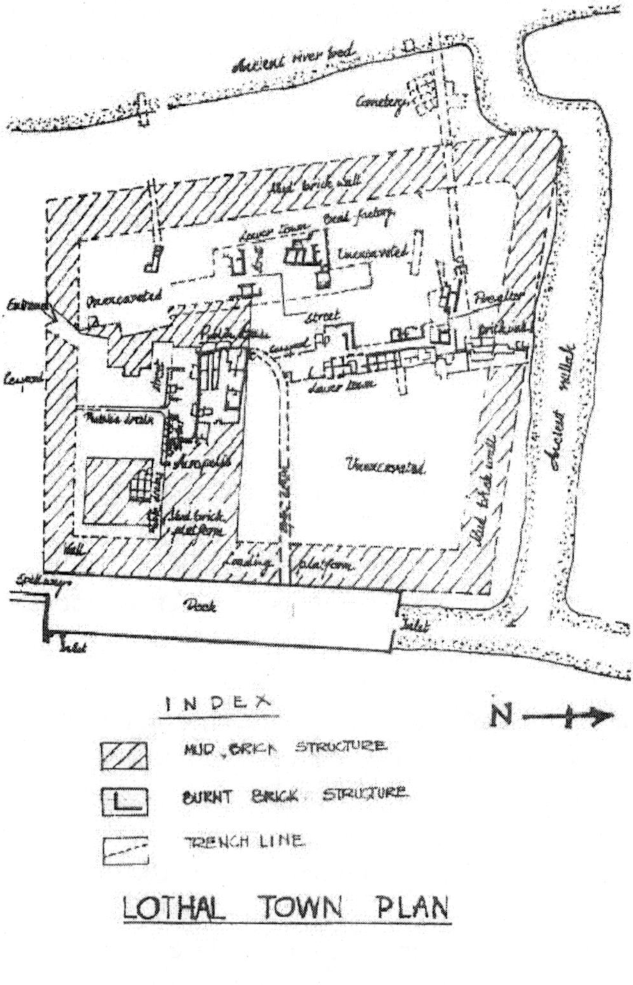

LOTHAL TOWN PLAN

The Architect: (STHAPATI) VASTUSHASTRA

It was strongly believed that he, who begins work as an architect (Sthapati), without knowing the science of architecture (Vastushastra), is proud with false knowledge, must be put to death by the king, as one who ruins the kingdom (Rajahimsaka); is dead before his time, and his ghost will wander on this wide earth.

He, though well-versed in the traditional science, if not skilled in the work, will faint at the time of action like a timid man on the battlefield.

He, who is expert only in his workmanship, but unable to understand the meaning of traditional science, will, like a blind man, be misled by anyone.

For immediate intuition, a readiness (Pratyupana) of judgment (Prajna) in contingencies, and ability to fuse them into the requirements of the whole, are the distinctions of a true Sthapati (architect).

The architect (Sthapati) along with his team of a draughtsman (Sustragrahi), carpenter (Takshaka) and mason (Vardhaki) had their origin from the four faces of Brahma (the Creator of the universe). Amongst these, the architect holds the key position. He should be well – versed in traditional sciences, perfect in body, righteous, kind, free from malice and jealousy. He should know the ancient compendia of myths etc... He should be joyous, truth speaking, concentrated in mind, free from greed, disease and the seven vices and having crossed the ocean of the science of Vastu (architecture). His team should also be highly competent in their own fields.

The Site

In the ancient text 'Samrangana Sutradhara', King Bhoja recounts the afflictions of men, when the wishing trees (Kalpadruma) which had been their home and sustenance, and when the Gods, too, whithdrew to heaven, it was then that King Prithu, the first of men, who was installed as king, attacked Prithvi, the earth, with his bow in order to level her, for she was full of mountains, obstacles to communications and order which he had set himself to establish. But she ran away in fear, changing her shape into that of a cow and took refuge with Brahma (the Creator), whom King Prithu had also approached. Brahma mediates between them, and makes her King Prithu, the protector of Prithvi, the earth, and makes her yield to him the crops and the sites for building towns of men and Gods.

Preparation of the Site

Before the construction of a new dwelling, the soil is ploughed, sowed with various seeds. After the germination, it is ploughed again. All this is done ensure the fitness and ritual purity of the site. For the same reasons, all extraneous matter (thorns etc.). Has to be removed from the soil, so that it doesn't stand in the way of the divinities. Its presence forebodes evil to the builder and is felt as an uneasiness and local irritation in various parts of the body.

After this, the site is to be stamped down by the cows, sanctified by their breath, purified by the contented lowing of the bulls and consecrated by the froth which flows from the mouth of the calves; it will be lastly consecrated by the sprinkling of holy water. Purity of the soil is most important. Night and before day break, when the ground is tilled, the past ceases to count; new life is entrusted to the soil and another cycle of production begins. The sowing of the grain is the final offering to the memory of the spirits who have left the place and the first offering to the newly acquired land. Their germination leads to the fulfilment of all their potentialities. The grain has the nature of the sacrificial essence itself, for it is said in 'Satapatha Brahmana' (an ancient text), from man, the sacrificial victim, this essence passes to the sacrificial animals, it entered into horse, goat, sheep, ox and lastly into the earth with its rice and barley.

Purification of Places

Before the performance of any ceremony, the place where it is to take place must be previously purified. This is usually the duty of women, and the principal ingredients required are cow dung and darbha grass. They dilute the cow dung with water and make a sort of plaster with it, which is spread over the floor with hands, making zigzags and other patterns with lime or chalk as they go on. Drawn then are wide lines of alternate red and white over this and sprinkled with darbha grass. (Refer to Diag. No. 4).

This is the way in which the Hindus purify their houses day by day from the defilement caused by promiscuous goers and comers. It is the rule amongst the upper classes to have their houses rubbed over once a day with cow dung, but in any class it would be considered as unpardonable and gross breach of good manners to omit this ceremony when they expect friends or go to receive company. (Refer to Diag. Nos. 5 & 6). & paint their house with white & green color, on entire door mark swastic with saffron color pattern with red color.

Materials

Bricks form the "body of the sacrifice" (Yajnatance). Detailed descriptions are given how to make good baked bricks, and this practical knowledge gained by experience accompanies a sacred memory (Smriti), a tradition by which the acquired technical skill became perfected.

The act itself of offering had gone into the making of the bricks. It is a rite of identification. The substance of the brick is its carrier; earth, water and five are the elements which take part in it. With reference to the 'Vedu Attar', it is thus known: "In fire, the fire gods bathed it by means of oblations: and whatever oblation they offered, became a baked brick and passed onto it and because they were produced from the offering (Ista), therefore, they are Istaka (bricks).

Earth brick made of earth shares the nature of the earth. What is required of he- is the steadiness and the firmness which is equally necessary to each layer of the monument (building) as it is raised up.

Dwellings in stone are suitable for the Brahmins and Kshatriyas, not forthe Vaisyas and Shudras. (Refer to Diag. No. 3)

The stone should be of uniform color, dense, smooth and deeply embeded in earth. It must be mature and of pleasing the stone licked by wind, sun or fire should be rejected. The architect should reject too soft a stone and the one which has been in alkaline water. He should reject one which is shaky or which has been displaced; one which is rough or which is discarded; one which has already been used. He should reject one with streaks, spots and flaws, one that is aged and crow grained, one which contains grit or which is of indefinite color, one with cracks, and one which is sound inside a building, one which gives off no sound.

Timber is the earliest building material. The tree having certain qualities only is chosen as building material. The chosen tree must be perfect, hard and vigorous. The tree should not be very old, dead or a sapling. It should not be crooked or damaged. It should be growing in a holy place, mountain, woods or river banks. The trees should be pleasing to eye and to mind. Such trees bring prosperity and good fortune. For building, tree is examined on the criteria of colors, taste and bark. The origin of trees, their place of growth affect the qualities of the tree, viz., and its strength and fibre growth. So, the trees which grow on the following places are unfit for building: cemetery, way or highway, tank or pool, hermitage, field, garden, boundary of town or village. Trees which grow on zig-zag round, shallow ground, bitter ground, soul full of acidity, soil of pungent or saltish taste should be discarded.

3

Vastu Shastra Programming in Vedic Architecture Tradition

Artists, Interior Designer & architects in India are inspired by the color graphics of Yantras and Mandala with special different colors. Some adopt this theory for their projects from this source. We will discuss in detail in this Chapter about the etymological roots of Mantra, Yantra, Tantra and the Vastu-Purusha. How & why they applied the color, and give more important to color science.

The Vedic concept describes the creation in two basic phenomena: Purusha and Prakriti.

PURUSHA is consciousness, the life source. It is also called Atman. The Paramatman or Vaishwanara (the universal consciousness), the Atman (individual consciousness), Prana (life) and Jiva (also life or soul). Paramatman and Atman are one, but represent two scales. Atman reflects as Prana or Jiva in the body through Mind. (According to Shiva Sankalpa Sutra, Mind in its purest Satvika form is itself Atman.) Purusha is timeless, ageless, constant, absolute consciousness. A singular truth – Adwaita. Prana is the central source of all energies in all living things, and not energy itself. Prakriti is the world of names and forms. Ever-changing, evolving and operating in Dwaita. (The Duals). The dualism of positive-negative, creation destruction, good-bad, male-female etc.

PRAKRITI has countless forms. The Prakriti also has permanence, but of a different nature. It is in the cyclic relay order, i.e., while the specie survives over the time, the body of the specie is created and destroyed and recreated again and again. So, at a given body level, it is temporary. After Prakriti comes Purusha, the life source. Purusha manifests itself in Prakriti through Ego and Ambition (Tamas and Rajas). Purusha Suktam of the Puranas describe this vivid play of Prakriti and Prursha in great detail. Thus, the Purusha is the life, the essence, the idea, the will behind any name or form – the physical world, in the absence of which the physical mass, forms or systems simply crumble and decompose. Purusha is the power behind all physical existence.

The Mind

Mind is the Lord and the author of Man's physical world around:

The Mind mainly operates at two levels. The external (convex) mind receives and reflects all information from the Prakriti–(The external world of names and forms). The physical world consists of five elements: Space, Air, Fire, Water, and Earth. These represent: Sound, Touch, Sight, Taste and Smell. The sense organs are the physical instruments through which Mind communicates with the physical world. Ordinarily, mind depends on the sense organs for communication with the physical world. Thus, the mind may be fed information as per the 'interests' or conditioning of the sense organs. The objectives of sense organs are Artha, Kama, and Dharma (Wealth, Comforts and Glory). The external surface of mind is in constant touch with the external world and its nature is to be mobile constantly, so as to efficiently perform its basic job to keep in touch with prakriti information and to transmit it, i.e. , to communicate.

The wandering mind is constantly in wants; desires, feeling of incompleteness. Always wanting, never satisfied. This makes man feel insecure, weak, lack of confidence, etc. So, man looks for psychological and moral support all the time, viz., support of any MEDIUM (religion, work, people, drugs, etc.)

The core Mind or the inner mind has the function of communicating with Purusha. However, unlike the external Mind, it does not depend on external physical sense instruments. This mind has to train itself to be self-operative. An untrained mind may feel this capacity at times, but cannot operate at will on this facility. Unlike Prakriti, Purusha is stable, timeless, ageless, continuous, pure consciousness, source of creativity, the beginning of all beginnings, life behind all Prakriti. The inner mind is introvert, quiet and meditative, a constant source of truth, solitude and happiness. The inner mind is made of 'Satvika' aspects of the five elements and sheaths (physical, emotional, intellectual, vital energy and bliss).

Its goal is to seek communication with Atman and Paramatman and merge with it when detached from the Mind-body complex. This mind never dies and has continued with time and space. The information collected, stored and processed by individual minds gets transmitted to the universal mind. There is constant two-way transmission between the two minds. One finds universal waves of similar thoughts at different time slots, affecting culture and behaviour of people over a large geographical region.

Human Problems

The human problems are of three kinds:

1. Two basic human desires. To procure the desired and to protect the procured. This is the constant source of the feeling of insecurity. (Ambition–Rajas)
2. If he can manage, he would wish to have it with no effort or minimum effort (Tamas).
3. The restless external mind is, time and again, reminded by the inner mind to hold, think, meditate, come back to the self, co-operate with the Purusha in the law of Prakriti. There is a constant struggle within the mind and creation.

Patanjali's Yoga Sutra

As solutions to the above problems, various answers or the view–points have evolved, called Darshanas. The Yoga Sutra avoids external mediums as far as possible (though does not bar them) and has developed Yoga technology and attitudes with the Mind – Body complex itself as medium and auto-suggestive methods. The schools are of little relevance for the purpose of evolving patterns for architectural expressions. However, it is mentioned for its importance in training of the designer's creative mental attitudes.

The Icons, Yantras and Mandals

These are for visual responses or codes. These are visual symbols as medium or invocation, icons or Murti or statues in human forms, semi-human, animal or demonic forms. These are most popular among the visual symbols for the common people. The iconic symbols range from a human figure representing the entire universe (Vaishvanara, Viratswarupa, etc.) to various other specific energy systems to be invoked for a particular objective, such as Shakti, Lakshmi, Saraswati, Brahma, Vishnu, Shiva, etc. each one with specific symbols is associated to represent the energies assimilated within the specific network.

Knowledge to Design or Create by Using Different Colors

Thorough understanding, right application and meaningful communication are important team work. In order to keep the total balance, it has to be very accurate.

For any activity, following are the three aspects:-

1. Mantra or Concept
2. Yantra or Mediums (instruments or tools)
3. Tantra or act of creation (administration)

The Mantras

Mantras are graphic symbols representing the respective energy networks. Each Yantra has its mantra as well as icon.

Shri mantra, Gayatri mantra, Surya, Yogini, Vishnu, etc. All Yantras evolve patterns form a central point. This centre is considered the source of creation and the object for concentration. The concentric patterns around the centre are specific to the energy pattern one wishes to invoke. This pattern is a visual code to constantly remind the Sadhaka of the network he is meditating on.

These are for audial responses or codes. It may be monosyllable like Om, Rim, Klim, Krim, Fat, etc. or in hymn form with the combination of sounds, words, dictions of specific composition to invoke a given set of energies by using different colors codes.

The Yantras

Yantras are for the intellectually superior or evolved persons who may not need icons. Yantras are generally two dimensional, symmetric, concentric patterns using elementary geometric forms such as circle, square and other regular geometric polygons. Lotus flowers varying from four to one hundred petals are also incorporated. Yantra can be designed and developed to represent any specific energy network. Yantras have different color codes, too.

Tantras (Karmakanda and Tantrism)

The problem is of the relationship between the sense organs and the external mind. The mind and the senses both should be disciplined and be in harmony and awareness with Prana. Mediums and methods are developed, responding to senses and the sensuality of Mind. First, the mind should have positive reasons and clear objectives to concentrate upon. To reach that state of stability, some intermediary medium-vehicles or catalysts-are developed. These carriers are sound, touch, vision, taste and smell, since; these are the factors of sense organs. The mediums or vehicles should correlate with the specific objective. It should have potency to reach the goal and its directions and action network to be with clear accurate commands. Mantras, Yantras and Tantras are developed with these considerations. In Sanskrit, these are defined as:

Protection through Mind is Mantra (Concept)

Protection through Effort is Yantra (Work)

Protection through Crossing (Hurdles) is Tantra (Management and Methods)

Mantra is for mental conceptual efficiency. Sound (audial form) is its vehicle.

Yantra is for work efficiency. Vision (Visual form) is its vehicle.

Tantra is for Management efficiency. Process is its vehicle.

Similarly, there are specific touch, taste and smells associated with specific Mantra, Yantra and Tantra.

The above three are MEDIUM and METHODS, bridging human WILL to objectives, designed and developed for various kinds of human desires – Material, Emotional, Intellectual, Vital, and bliss-Tamasika, Rajasika or Satvika. While these medium are used to help a Sadhaka to attain intial meditation practice, these are more popular among the common people as methods to attain material goals of life. For the second group of goals, one is interested in satisfying certain specific desires such as procure and protect, wealth, comforts, glory, sensual or mental gratification, etc. for each of these, the MEDIUM are utilized to invoke specific set of energies in a desired pattern of network and potency.

Architecture

As per the Oxford Dictionary, architecture is derived from the Greek word 'ARCHITEKTON'.

Arch - Chief, also, Arch – consciously playful and Teasing Tekton – Builder. (Technique, Technology).

One can develop that the architect is the Chief Builder, consciously evolving playful and pleasing environment. He is the master of art of building.

Vitruvious, the Greek theoretician, defined three qualities of architecture.

Utility: Stability: Colorful Environment

One may also derive:

Archi – Tec – Ture = Playful – Technology – Culture = A culture of building playfully.

Thus, architecture incorporates:

COMMODITY– Real Estate, Investments, Comforts of Living, Shelter, Activities and Utility.

Protection against: weather, undesired elements such as insects, strangers, animals, etc.

Yet keeping meaningful contact with the Elements of Nature, Views, Society.

STABILITY: Strength, Durability, Maintenance

DELIGHT–Visual, Audio, Smell, Temperature and Taste (Perceptions).

Moods, Emotions, Intellect, Vitality and Bliss.

These are psychological and aesthetical dimensions of Commodity and Stability.

Buildings must be comfortable and strong and must feel so, too. Must give psychological satisfaction, too.

Above all, architecture is the culture of building playful joyous environments. Like any culture, it expresses life and grows over a long span of time. Architecture is seen, felt, perceived, conceived and experienced. Architecture is extension of man in all its sense manifestations under given human activities.

Ruskin called architecture as Mother of all arts.

Color painting is two dimensional arts and sculpture is three dimensional art, as viewed from outside.

Architecture has fourth dimension: Interior. It is lived in and is experienced from inside as well as outside.

Luis I kahn said "ARCHITECTURE IS MAKING THOUGHTFUL SPACES." Within and around buildings.

MAN, Society and Culture are subjects. Technology, Mediums of Construction tools. Land and environment are form givers.

To transform living, life and ideas into architectural realities is our profession.

Architecture expands into Habitat, Urban Design, Landscape Design and Urban Planning. At micro scale, it involves Interior Design, Product Design and Graphic Design, give more importance to colors.

Design, thus, is a very versatile field.

Art of Building

In the Indian (Hindu) system, the art of building is defined into two groups:

Vastu Kala

Derived from the Sanskrit word "VAAS" meaning to reside. It mainly deals with human habitation and houses. It is concerned with physical comforts, community and privacy, social structure, security, commodity, etc. A Vaastukar is a master builder –A Raj Mistry. Indian thought considers the physical and the metaphysical as inseparable union. Thus, the orientation of the house, the dimensions of the house, spaces, etc. were derived from the horoscope of the owner, matched with location and Vastu-Purusha. Design of the entrance gate, number of open courts, sequencing of spaces, scale of the spaces and the artistry in the craft of the building elements, all reflected social status, cast, ritualistic and belief systems, family systems, etc. there are seven Vastu Shastras in India practised in different parts of the country. Each one developed separately for a respective agro-climatic and eco-cultural zone. Some of these are: Raj Vallabh, Samarangana Sutradhar, Aparajita Prichchha, Maya Matam, Manasara, Kautilya Shastra.

Sthapatya Kala

Derived from the Sanskrit word "Sthapa" to establish, to set the cardinal directions. Sthapatya kala deals with buildings of celestial permanence. Temples - the house of the God. Since the King also represented the Lord, the royal palaces were also attended by the Sthapati (The architect).

If mathematics is the ultimate expression of the conceptual arts, sciences and philosophies, all perceptual and exotic expressions culminate in architecture.

Later, the institutions of merchant, priest, education, wealth, administration, etc. also have been attended by Sthapati. These are more permanent in nature and universal in expression. However, strictly speaking, these full under Vastu Kala, since these have human purposes. So, Vastu-Sthapatya.

The establishment of Vastu-Purusha in temple design has relative differences, the direction of its axis, its plan form, plinth, walls, Shikhara. Vastu Purusha for physical human in functions considers physio -psychic aspects of site and design.

In the West, in Islamic and Christian architecture, where the construction medium has been stone, it may have originally evolved as a structural form.

But ever since Renaissance period in Europe, Persia or India (14th to 17th century), the structural dome and the visual dome have been two distinct elements. It is the structural basic form of arch, the cone is the basic form of the structural dome. The visual domes are either constructed over the inner conical shell or a segmental shell. (Refer to the Domes of St. Peters, Rome; The Mosque of the Shah at Isfahan; (Humayun's Tomb or Taj Mahal, India.) Also, this elaborate construction of the visual or symbolic dome is seen mainly over the churches, mosques or mausoleums-the buildings for spiritual or religious purposes.

The Hindu architecture restricted its technology mainly to Trabeated construction, mainly Corbelling. The construction spans restricted almost to flat or semi-flat roofs. Here, we find 'Chhatri' the most vividly and enchanting elements of the building and urban skyline. The Chhatri found its place at four corners of buildings or even at one corner, as a symbolic gesture. On gateway and even the minarets (Taj Mahal). The CHHATRI is explained in the Shastras as symbolic of man's relation with the cosmos. The form is the composition created out of the visual symbols of the five elements: Space, Air, Fire, Water and Earth, of which the physical universe is made. The combination form is highlighted as a very important elements, as the crowning of the building; as well as the urban skyline. In India, the Samadhis/mausoleums of Hindu Kings or important people may only be a Chhatri or composition of Chhatri. Color play a very important role of design & decoration.

4

Vedic Vastu: Architecture of Five Elements (Earth, Air, Water, Fire & Space)

Man is the subject, object and cause of architecture. He perceives and conceives architecture in relation to his experiences of himself with the surrounding world.

As a tool making animal, he designs and controls his environment and buildings. They, by the environmental changes created by him to suit his choices of living, directly reflect his personal, social, material, emotional, intellectual and vital personalities.

Through act of design, he alters and moulds the elements of natural environment. The sequences of the natural elements when used as "The Materials" of architecture reverse as follows:

Earth, Water, Air, Sun and Space. (From physical to etherial). Earth and water have limited and localised availability for human habitat and growth. Since earth and water have cognizable physical body, they form apparent and fundamental choice makers in the location and the physical form of architecture and habitat. Though Sun, Air, and Space also form select priorities for comfortable human life, apparently these are universally available and can be moulded to human needs by the act of design by earth and water. Among all these, water is shy element. Habitat, therefore, foes where water is. Only in some very special situations, water is diverted to habitat. But this decision often expensive and not feasible, economically and ecologically. (Fatehpur Sikri could not be inhabited for non-availability of water.)

Ideal habitats, cultures, architecture and life have naturally shown exhilarence where all the five physical elements to support life are abundantly available and are suitable to human growth and evolution. The oldest, the rich and the living cultures and civilizations all over the globe have been along the temperate zones, i.e., the Zone of Cancer and the Zone of Capricorn, where the evolution of human mind reached its peak at the earliest. The recorded period of the present history goes back to 5000 years, when one knows that about 4000 years ago, in these regions, the human super minds lived. In other regions, such as Equator or the colder regions, civilizations and cultures developed later. In order to understand the act of design with these five physical elements, we shall take each one separately to appreciate their meaning, role and workability in architecture. For the present, broadly, they form their scope for human habitat as follow:

Earth: Land structure, Land form, Landscape, Flora and Fauna. It also establishes availability of local construction materials and their workability.

Water: The habitat and physical life are where water exist. This is true for all life forms and eco-culture. The type, form and pattern of life also greatly depend on relationship of earth and water. The sea front, river front, Lake Front, the underground water level or streams for wells are also important for flora to grow. Water is not the only life source, but is surely fundamental to location and growth of habitats.

Air: As a life supporting elements, air is very powerful life source. Two minutes of blockage of air supply to respiratory system can smother life. Pure air with oxygen is good for brain and blood. Human physical comfort values are directly and sensitively dependent on correct humidity, air flow, temperature of air, air pressure, air composition and its content. In this respect, air deals with the entire body surface through skin, respiratory and blood system-through respiration. Building systems, to handle air for comfort conditions, have direct impact on the form and visual qualities of architecture and habitats. Air also represents movement.

Fire (Sun): A source of mental energy. Best minds evolve in a natural process where the sun was temperate. Not very hot, not very cold, just the right temperature (+ or -3°) of 24°c The **hot sun** has glare, sharp light and **cool sun** rarely rises above horizon or often geographically coupled with heavy clouds in the sky and snow on earth. Generally gloomy but beautiful, silvery and long hours of twilight. Hot humid zones with heavy cloudy sky for longer periods of the year also have distinctive culture and architecture. Sun has played an important role in the development of visual qualities of architecture in terms of textures, color, roof, forms, and above all expression of vitality.

Space: All the above elements are skillfully engineered towards the creation of physically comfortable, emotionally pleasant, intellectually determinant, totally vibrant and blissfully satisfying spaces for human shelter and habitat. Man lives in space.

The main architectural rule for planning is orientation.

The architectural space is stimulated by the act of design for development and expression of the TOTAL MAN (Diag. No. 8)

In the following discussions, we shall elaborately deal with each one of these natural elements as "Architectural Medium".

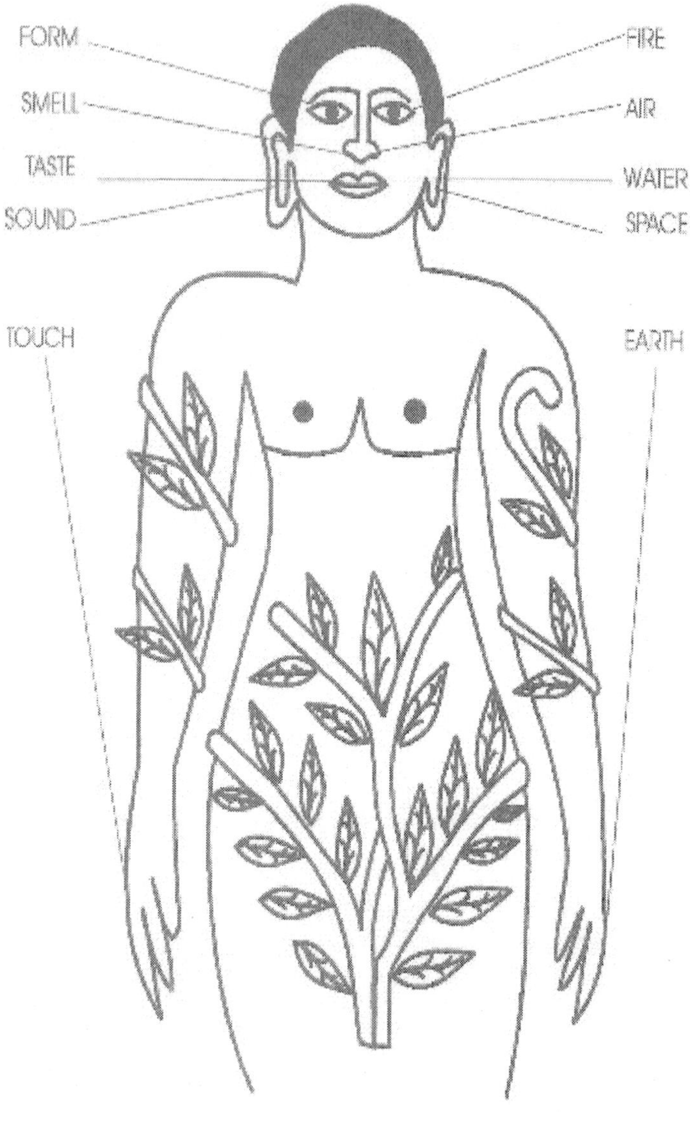

Monolithic Statue of Gometeshwar in Situ Granite

Diag. 8

A. 1.	Five Reflective Instruments of Perception (Physical/Mental):	Ears	Skin	Eyes	Tongue	Nose
2.	Architectural/Environmental:	Accoustics Vibrations	Climatology H.V.A.C.	Lighting	Water supply (Aesthetics) Color Texture Form Visuals	Appropriate Smells to Related Activities
B. 1.	Five Universal Activities:	Communicate	Work	Movement	Discard	General
2.	Reflective Work Organs (Physical):	Speech	Hands	Legs	Anus	Genitals
3.	Architectural or Environmental Transfers	Design Language Systems	Function Efficiency Systems	Circulation Systems	Sewerage (Judiciary)	Generative Systems
C. 1.	The Mind or Energy:	Physical	Emotional	Intellectual	Vital	Blissful
2.	Architectural Transfers:	Non-Measurable Dimensions Depicting Mental Comforts	Eco	Culture	Time	Space From

From the table given, one can clearly see: (A) How the various aspects of the physical body, senses, mind and their related manifestation in humanities, science and technology become interactive, relative, overlapping and integrated. (B) It also shows how the sciences of dimensioning emerge from the process.

One must realise at the outset that the Design language (more complex in Architecture and Habitat Design) is unique. Remember the following at all time:

1. It is very essential to learn to think, perceive, conceive experience, act and produce, all simultaneously. Design is not a linear process. All linear tools of expression such as speech, writing, etc. fall to express this simultaneously. One should be able to think, Observe, Analyse, sketch, design, all in a simultaneous process.
2. Man, surroundings and methods are integral to one another. They form a kind of universe within a universal system. Any Design action is, therefore, relative and requires Holistic, Meditative and Creative processes.
3. Similarly, Nature, Man and Product are within an evolutionary network. The Design process in this network is guided by performance standards which, again, are within the holistic framework, and therefore relative to a given situation.

5

Color of Vastu Mandla

Mandala means configuration, enclosure or network. Energy networks of desired objective are also expressed graphically in the matrix form in square, triangular, hexagonal or octagonal grids. The square grid is most common. (Astrological matrix of the donor or deity, the number combinations, the Yantra and also Mantra symbols are inscribed in specific configurations responding to respective network.) Mandala is particular to time, place, person and purpose. It is a composite operative programme chart of all necessary overlays, as explained below.

To sum up, the Mantra, Yantra and Mandala have science, technology and management techniques for discipline of mind for specific persons. They are in the holistic tradition of Vedic science and thoughts.

Vastu–Purusha–Mandala

Purusha and Mandala are associated with Vastu (site). Vastu means site, the site for building a house, or a dwelling. Vastu encompasses the house with site and its environment.

According to the Vedic thought, Purusha is not only the cause and life behind all Prakriti, but also behind all creations of Man. Since Mind, in its Satva form, represents Purusha and Mind is the Lord or author of all creations of Man – psychic as well as physical creations.

Any tool developed through human will, mind and effort is the extension of man himself. Whether as producer, receiver and user, man enjoys or suffers the development or limitedness of human intelligence or skill. So, the concept is that the man-made products are projections of his own personality (material, emotional, intellectual, and vital and bliss). The object made by him also has purusha (Atman or Prana).

The Spirit of the Building

The house is ruled by a demi-god, the 'Vastupurusha'. If not appeased, he would destroy the house and bring adverse conditions for the householder. To appease him, one must follow the sacred ceremonies at every step religiously. These rituals give sanctity to the entire process. The rituals and fasting to be followed by the architect help him gain full control over his mind, Body and soul. (Refer to Diagram No.1)

According to the text 'Mayamata', "It should be known that the spirit of the building (Vastupurusha) has six bones, a single heart, four vulnerable points and four vessels, and that he lies upon the ground, his head towards the north-east. "He, who, in every human dwelling, is responsible for good and for bad fortune that is why the wise must avoid tormenting his limbs with the limbs of the owner of the house. Thus, the sage must always spare the body of the spirit in the course of construction. If, through ignorance of the architects, any of its several parts be rendered defective, the master himself becomes completely ruined.

According to the text 'Brihat Samhita', the plots assigned to Brahma and other superior deities should not be polluted by throwing remains of food and other refuse on them. The gods are settled on the 'Vastupurusha'. Every building activity means a renewed conquest of disintegration, and at the same time a restitution of integrity so that the gods once more are the limbs of 'Vastupurusha' and must be appeased at every new undertaking in connection with the building, which he will have to carry. He is the Lord of the building and the earth is the mistress of the house. She is the soil. On her, he leaves his impression and she receives his seed. This is the meaning enacted in the rites of sowing the seeds. This is the meaning enacted in the rites of sowing the seeds.

The 'Vastupurusha', once laid on the ground , is measured out in squares, from east to west, with the course of the sun, from light to darkness; their total is 'Vastupurusha' Mandala of 64 or 81 squares. 45 Gods occupy his body, the extent of which differs but not their relative position in the plan, so is said in 'Brihat Samhita'. (Refer to Diag. No.2)

Vastu is primarily the planned site of the building. Its shape is square. It is the extent of existence in its ordered state and is beheld in the likeness of the purusha. The image of the super- natural or cosmic man, the Purusha, is congruous and identical to the planned site. Purusha, cosmic man, the origin and source of 'Apara Prakriti' (existence) is instrumental or efficient cause.

The plan makes the site of the building in his image, which is his form.

The plan of the building is in the likeness of the 'Purusha' or the totality of the manifestation. Mandala denotes any closed polygon. The form of 'Vastupurusha Mandala' although a square can be converted to triangle, circle, hexagon, octagon of equal area.

Man's total existence has three aspects: 'Adhyatmica' – the inner self, will, ego, prana and life energies, 'Bhowtika' – the physical social, environmental and material, and "Daivika' – the energies beyond man. The universal, global and cosmic, from which he invokes the energies within him and from which he should safeguard too. Man is governed by them. Through Vastupurusha Mandala, man also incorporates these aspects in the building. Thus, the Vastu Yantra and Vastupurusha Mandala are the creative conceptual diagrams which

"BRIHAT SAMHITA"

GANDHARVA

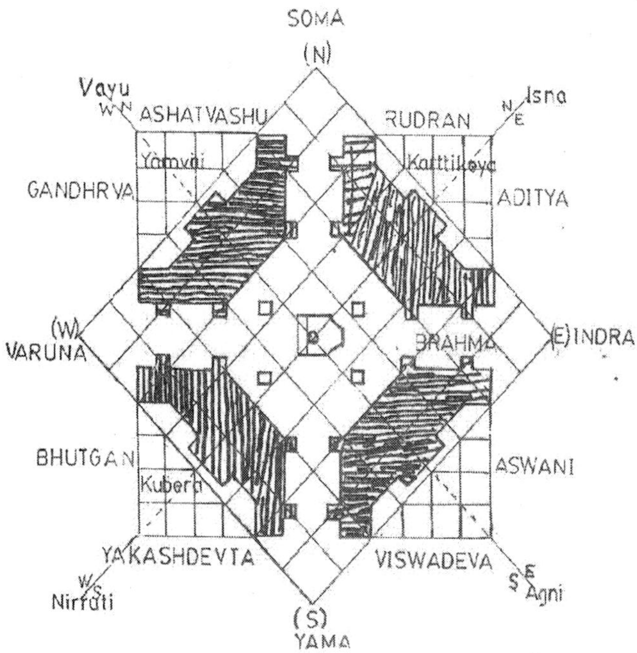

Vastupurusha Mandala 64 — Square (Pada)

Diag. 2

programme the building for the said three behavioral and protective aspects. Its language is symbolic. (Like any computer programme diagram or matrix). Since Vastupurusha Mandala is specific to time, place, and function and owner of the project, it is developed on a case-to-case basis.

We do find thought processes in the modern Western world similar to the Vedic thoughts. Luis I Kahn's theory of 'Ina'- the existence will of any object, his teachings about idea, form, design have similar process as the concepts of Purusha, mantra, Yantra, Tantra. Buckminister Fuller's Synergy-Energy concept is probably one of the purest energy Mandalas in 3D used to achieve any span of structural energy Mandalas in 3D used to achieve any span of structural enclosure. Frank Lloyd Wright's teachings on 'Unity from the door knob to the town plan-the Concept of Organic Architecture' are some of the famous parallels similar to the Vedic thoughts, only to mention a few.

The Vedic Mandala tries to overlay these various conceptual sieves on one Mandala. It is possible to cast such elaborate Mandalas for modern architecture with the help of the science of computers (artificial intelligence). The human mind is potentially the most original, efficient and creative than computer. The schools of creative arts and sciences in India have a storehouse of knowledge at their disposal, both for training of creative and productive minds as well as development of thought processes and methods to produce eco-culturally appropriate living environment.

Man, above all, is a tool making animal. He communicates and expands beyond his physical frame through mind, spirit, skills and instrumentations. This quality of man needs to be guided for positive co-existence. His various faculties be trained and disciplined for the highest efficiency, positive co-existence and creative efforts. The creative by comes with the help of different color scheme.

Now, let us understand the Nature-Man-Architecture transfer process. If man is a reflection of Nature, Architecture reflects Man and his total personality (Purusha). If human body and mind complex are instruments which communicate, expand and get consumed in the nature, Architecture and Habitat also pulsate, absorb, expand and get consumed into man. Nature, Man and Architecture (Habitat) are the natural evolutionary extensions of one another, forming a complete whole.

6

Art of Planning As per Vastu Science

Functions, Activities and Places

It is important to understand the scope and meaning of terms:

Functions, Functional, Activities, etc.

The Body-Mind is an auto-system. Man takes his sustenance, growth and development from colorful Nature.

The mind generates desires, aspirations and needs. It simultaneously activates the intellect within it, the sense organs and the work organs to GET or CONSTRUCT the desired object or input from the surrounding environment. (Natural and Human Systems).

He invents necessary tools, techniques and medium. Thus, the FUNCTIONS and ACTIVITIES incorporate all the three levels:

- Human desire or aspiration level
- Tools and techniques level
- Environment and medium level

Functioning at Human Aspiration Levels

Man has various existence roles. For each of his role, he has environmental needs to live or perform these roles. He wishes to perform each of his activities his way. He has his own way of ENJOYING work or acts, (joy of doing something). His own SANCTITIES. The way he sleeps, bathes, eats, works as a "Self" an individual, family, institution, etc. there are overtones and priorities of various issues such as Physical, Material, Emotional, traditions and taboos, aspirations, status or anonymity, intellectual, etc. thus, a simple act of Sleep, Eat, Cook, Meet, Sing, and the thousand other everyday activities have various environmental needs, desires or aspirations which give different meaning to different people 'FUNCTIONS' and 'ACTIVITIES', thus, assume much wider meaning.

The Habitat consists of the following FUNCTIONAL environmental pockets. These may be the entire town or city has single central function.

Each functional pocket of a habitat has its own architectural ambience, theme and expressions, symbols, moods and efficiency parameters. In a living organism such as Architecture or Habitat, each function has its own place, articulations, overlaps, transitional spaces and link spaces. There are streets squares, sequences, and climaxes of spaces, forms, activities and times.

In the individual buildings or rooms too, the functional spaces are of various kinds. These broadly fall under the following types:

1. Private Spaces
2. Public Spaces
3. Circulation Spaces
4. Service Spaces
5. Symbolic Spaces

In India, building designs very significantly from place to place. Regional and sub-regional differences in house design and building systems are quite obvious to the eye. There are flat roofed houses built in stone found in Rajasthan and sloping roof structures in bamboo in the North-East. North to south, there is also much diversity. This variety is the result of building system by a large number of people. 1) Living patterns, spatial and functional requirements, 2) Climate, 3) Economic Conditions of house and community, 4) Material and energy resources available, 5) Local building materials available, and 6) Codes, formal and informal standards. Color scheme as per Climate & Local Tradition.

Living patterns evolve due to a wide variety of influences, aspirations and the actual means of a family. Climate is constant over a very long period of time and lasts longer than the life-cycle of buildings. The economic strength of a family or community determines their ability to afford better shelter.

Utilization of available materials and energy resources in an area is something that building technologists have much greater control over. They can choose from existing resources and techniques of construction or develop new building materials, products and processes from locally available materials. They have the option of enlarging the resource base by importing materials from outside the locality. Building activity can also develop into a rural industry and contributes to the economic well-being and development of an area. The choice of technology is important in housing and, thus, developmental concerns must not be forgotten.

Housing is people's activity. We must recognize that it exists as a system today with its own dynamics. It is, however, a relatively unhealthy system and therein lies the problem. People are forced to put to other solutions from within the confines of their limited resources and abilities. More often than not, these are obsolete and short-lives. The solution to improving the state of shelter lies not re-designing the housing system, but we need to trigger off a process of technical selection and up gradation, as a result of which building systems are developed on the principal of solar effect building design.

Functions	Environmental/Architectural/ Habitat Resource	Predominant Functional Quality
1. Self	Deeper privacy cell. A private Articulated corner or a room.	Self, meditative secure from social Invasions unless permitted Occasionally.
2. Family	House, Home, Flat. (Home houses man's As temple houses God.) It has	Family interactive functions within its ethnic, economic and social contracts. Often, also a place of work for Economic survival.
3. Casteor Group	Mohalla, housing, Apartment, block, Institutional housing, Dormitory, towns. town. (Manaas, "people" find their roots in Mohalla. There is a seed, space which Identifies it.)	Group interactive, among houses Within and with other Mohallas in festivals and rituals were performed together. The mohalla or housing, as a Whole, has specific group ethnic Ambience.
4. Trade & Exchage Services and Goods (Retail)	Market, Mandies, tertiary and functional services, social information exchange points (A pan corner, barber's shop, Halwai corner or Golgappa corner, etc.)	Markets and Mandies are represented by Trade Guilds or Trade Associations. Central Functional Markets are the Exchange of goods, services and "News". It has trade symbols.

5. Commercial Centers	Commercial Offices and Establishments.	Generation of money and wealth.Is has "Material" ambience representing culture of entrepreneurs.
6. Work, Industry	Varying from cottage industries with crafts and work, to small-scale and high-tech industries, Warehousing, etc.	Production process and work disciplines, efficiency and dignity of Labour "Prestige of the product". "Hands are the makers of Man's Material destiny."
7. Political Power and Administration	Civic complexes, Spaces and Building, Government Offices, Capital Towns.	Power, Governance in Democratic or Autocratic form. Spaces for people's representations & political meetings. (The scale and culture of governance).
8. Education, Health, Sots	Schools, Universities Educational Towns, Hospitals, Health Resorts and Sanatoriums, Research centers, Sports and Health Centers.	Perseverance and development of Human Mind and Body. Intellectual work efficiency, human service with Grace. Also, conservation and generation of information. Togetherness for learning, exchange of ideas, development of philosophies, evolution of psyche.

9. Religion and Culture	Culture Centers, temples, Ashrams, spiritual Resorts at Sensitive Ecological Spots.	Repose, search of inner voice, Meditation. Sprouting of life forms in Various forms: music, dance, theatre, paintings, experiencing bliss, self-evolution.
10. Recreation	Theatres, cinema halls, clubs restaurants and Associated activities.	Pleasurable "fun" sports, as well as Culturally flavored. It is different from 'Culture' as it has commercial viewpoint with material ambience. Exhibitionism.
11. Mobility and Movements	Circulation systems in buildings and town. circulation nodes such as Lobby, Squares.	Mobility is the life of buildings and habitats. The connect various Railway station, Bus terminus, Airport, Jetty, Seaport. Functional spaces, moods and scales. The "Circulation Architecture" holds the various functions and expressing Together (Experiencing movement in space is Architecture!)

1. Fulfill functional requirement of the building element
2. More cost-effective
3. Energy-effective (green building's)
4. Material which is economical and ecological
5. Trained manpower (Local available)

Energy is being wasted or used excessively in many building products and techniques when confronted with a problem of cost. Most people prefer, due to attitude, to pay more instead of attempting to optimize the building system.

There is enormous scope to innovate over the entire range of building systems so that wastefulness is reduced and long-term development concerns are kept in mind with cost reduction. Prefabrication of certain building elements is an obvious necessity. Mud Architecture is also an alternative method.

7

Eco-friendly Vastu or Vedic Architectural Mediums

Building Materials (Mediums), Form and Structure

Before the industrial revolution, 5000 years of architectural development used only three basic materials, Mud-Bamboo, Clay-Bricks Tiles, Stones and Wood. Today, a flood of new building materials are seen in the market.

A. Conventional

1.	Natural Rock: Stones, clay, bricks, tiles. (Bricks & tiles are included here since these are used for the last 5000 year and so naturalized with man. Also, their processing is within the normal human "day –to-day techniques of Banking".)	Granular Structure
2.	Wood and Organic Manufactured Materials: Natural Timber, Plywood, Fibre Board, Laminated Wood, etc.	Cellular or Cross-cellular Fibrous Structure
3.	Metals & Alloys: All metal extractions Form mineral ores with very high Temperature.	Granular or flaked metallurgical structures

4. Synthetic: Plastics, Resins, Glass, etc.	As per chemical structures. (Thermo-plastics and Thermo-Static).
5. Hybrid: Made by mixing two or more Materials may be from different "Families".	Hybrid, such as concrete, R.C.C., etc.
6. Color all synthetic material	

B. Non-Conventional

Mud, Ash, Dust of Burnt Bricks, Bamboo, Lime and Clay: & Natural Organic color.

The natural materials do extend warmth and go well ecologically with Man. Technologically, they have several limitations, such as, dimensional Availability and relative cost, structurally less economical as their strength per unit load has to have higher safety factor due to possible natural defects such as loose grains, roughs or knots, etc. Also, actual good building quality material from the trees or quarries has to be very selective; so uneconomical. Manufactured goods such as plywood, block boards, metals, synthetics etc. are designed metallurgically or through physical manufacturing processes to take pre-determined loads. So, structurally, these are economical. They can take more loads in smaller sectional dimensions. No wastage was available in pre-determined standards. They are, sleek, a typical character of modern technological products. Natural color made from vegetable & natural material.

The choice of materials is done on the basis of pre-determined parameters:

Visual textures, colors, workability, strength, availability and durability and maintenance requirements. These are variable.

Materials of various families or mass contents have varying co-efficient of expansion, varying absorption of heat or moisture, varying durability, workability and maintenance requirements. Mixing them as a hybrid materials or joining them as building systems requires careful handling. This understanding about compatibility of the materials of different types is very important to build "healthy" buildings. Such buildings are durable, need less maintenance and are visually satisfying.

When we look at the history of construction, the most rudimentary form of covering a space or an opening in a wall was to place a timber log or a stone beam over the two supports at its end. The earliest examples are the stone hangs.

Later, the ancient civilizations and cultures of Mesopotamia, Egypt, Maya, Persia, India, Greece, etc. developed some of the most exquisite examples of architecture in this method of construction.

The Rectangular or CUBIC FORMS emerging from this system are known as TRABEATED FORMS.

It is a GRAVITY CONSTRUCTION SYSTEM. Here, the span to be covered is equal to the length of the material covering it.

The visual forces of the architectural compositions follow the structural forces. Thus, in the gravity constructions, the basic visual expressions are: the forces of vertical lines of the supporting columns, such as in the Greek fluted columns; or on the Egyptian gateway walls expressing the vertical transformation of stress to the ground from the heavy roof lines or the entablature.

The Indian temple styles

OR

The composition in horizontal lines expressing building layer in the solid stones as found in the South Indian and

Orissan temples interestingly add to visual lightness of otherwise physically heavy buildings.

Limitations of Trabeated Construction

Some basic limitations are:

1. Material handling
2. Very low weigh-span ratio
3. Expensive, high costs of large sizes of building materials
4. Non-availability of wood or good stone at many geographical locations

Need to Develop Roofing Systems

Out of the stones used for walls:

For masonry and brick walls, small workable sizes of bricks and stones were standardized. We have records of 5000 years' old history from MOHENJODARO.

The criteria were:

1. Easy grip within the palm and fingers of the Mason.
2. Easy to lift and set with one hand while making the masonry.
3. Easy to transport within, say, 30-40 meters on the site by the head loads of 8-12 bricks.
4. Proper burning in case of the bricks, wall masonry work is done at great heights standing on narrow scaffoldings. Materials are also lifted at these heights by physical human

labour. So, for wall masonry, small sizes of stone slabs or cubes were cut.

A method of gravity construction called CORBELLING was developed for spanning the wall openings and the roofing systems to cover spaces, with masonry bricks and stones.

Corbelling

Here, the wall opening or the Space between the four walls Is covered by projecting the Layers of stones or bricks Successively till they meet at A point.

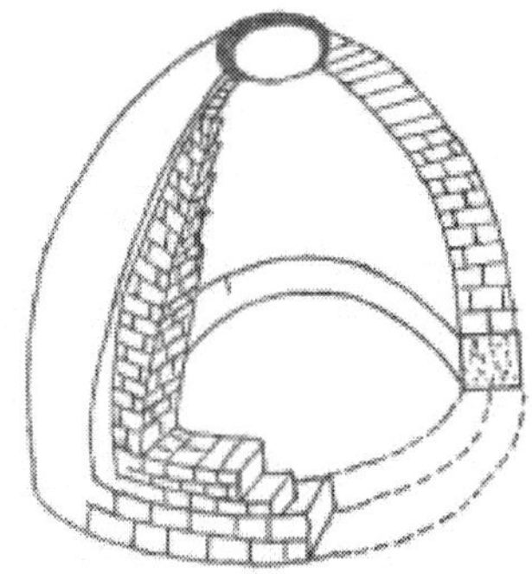

Generally, of the stone or Bricks length is projected Beyond The grip of the wall Bonding. Thereby, the CENTRE OF GRAVITY is Maintained within the wall, And the projected part does not fall off. The day's work is Stopped when the Centre of Gravity gets beyond the stability point. The further work starts after the previous corbels have set and hardened.

Corbels were treated differently by DIFFERENT CULTURES.

The Hindu culture treated them in the natural stepped format or in TORANA bracket forms as decorative.

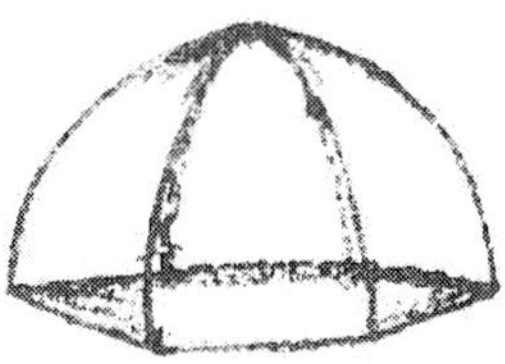

The square base of temples was lifted in the same square profile to become shikharas.

When the Shikhara had to be short, They used the technique of CROSS CORBELLS.

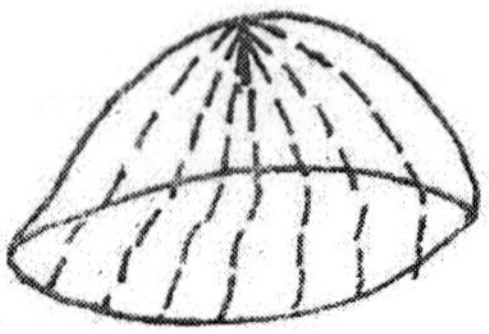

Temple was conceived as a small meditation cell and itself a symbol of God as an External form. Only Trabeated or corbelled systems were used as construction method. When large temples were to be built, the system failed. The famous Temple of SUN at Konark could never be completed as it started sinking in found and developed major cracks while almost completed.

External form. Only Trabeated or corbelled systems were used as construction method. When large temples were to be built, the system failed. The famous Temple of SUN at Konark could never be completed as it started sinking in found and developed major cracks while almost completed.

The Corbelling Systems of the Muslim Culture

The Islamic culture treated the CORBELLING SYSTEM as development of GRAVITY ARCHES, DOMES and VAULTS.

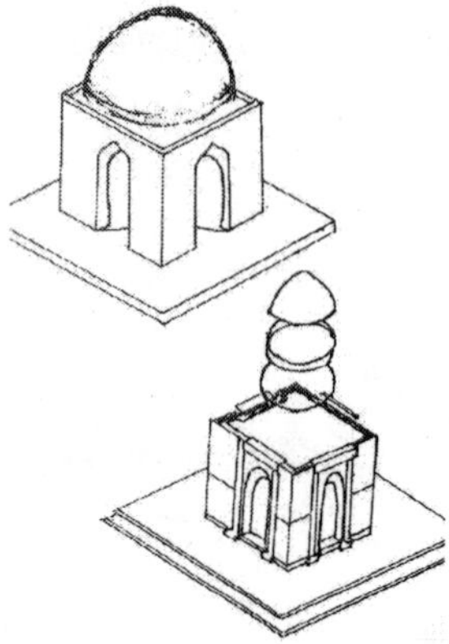

This has given very peculiar shape and proportions to their Arches and Domes.

It may be noted that when an arch rotates along its vertical axis, it becomes a DOME. When the arch moves along its horizontal span, it becomes a VAULT. Thus, in principle, Arches, Vaults and Domes of the SAME STRUCTURAL PRINCIPLES have similar FORM EXPRESSIONS.

One does find Pyramidical Roof, Conical Roof or Domes in Islamic buildings. Often centering was used to CAST vaults in random rouble stones and lime mortar. Muslim Vaults, therefore, are not always truly corbelled vaults.

Corbelling of Domical Roof gad four stages:

1. The Square base
2. The placing of diagonal stones at the corners to turn Square, to Octagonal base to sixteen-sided base to circular base.
3. The circular cylinder as dome base.

4. The series of successively corbelled rings of stones progressively becoming an onion like dome.

Christian Corbelling Forms

The Christian Europe rarely used the corbelling system in a major way. However, often the circular turret corner of the medieval or Renaissance period had conical corbelled roof.

The Christian System of Arches, Vaults and Domes

The Arch

Unlike the CORBELLED constructions, The Arches are not gravity system.

When two stones were hoisted in a 'pitched' form against each other to support an opening, to support an opening, they surely could take a span larger than 3 meters.

But the central pitch of the two stones tended to fall down to ground due to gravity force.

This created side-ward THRUST a horizontal component of the gravity force (vertical force).

But the stones stayed in position, because the base of the span on both the sides withstood the horizontal PUSH or thrust. If the base gave away due to the push, the ARCH ACTION would have failed, and the stones would have fallen down.

The arch action is the system of the vertical force of gravity at the CROWN of the Arch with its horizontal component of thrust at the Base of the arch, resulting in COMPRESSIVE FORCE SYSTEMS.

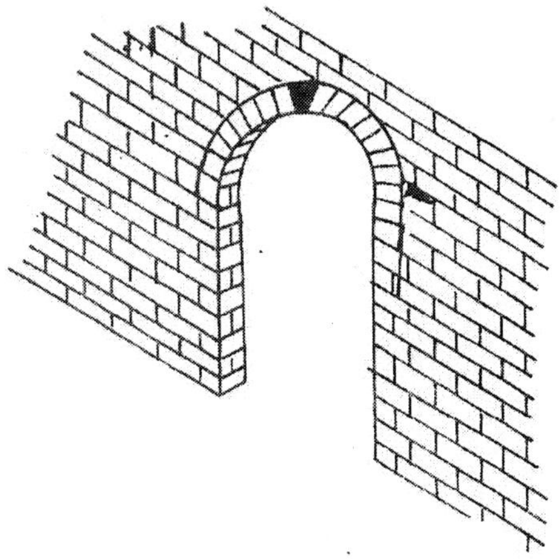

This principle of thrust was further refined with the building bricks or stone blocks used for wall construction.

The Round Arch

The two stones earlier had essentially a WEDGE SHAPE to get support surfaces.

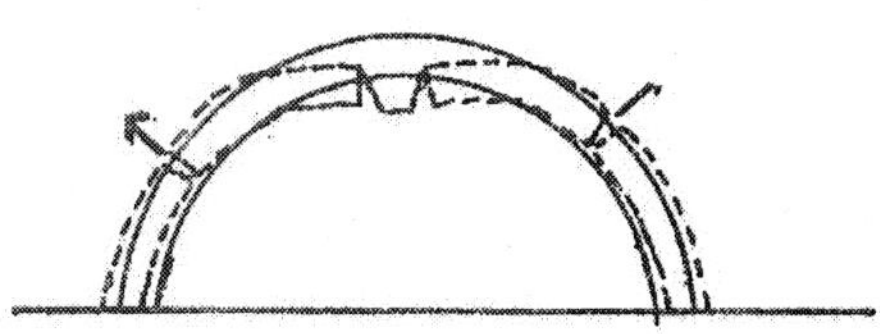

The smaller stones were cut to wedge shape to follow a radius in arch, using Zebra contrast to express the shaped stones like Turkish arches, stepping up or down the arch so fit, emphasizing by ornamentations around the series of arches.

The Vaults

When the arch travels along right angle to its span, it makes a BARREL VAULT. Since the barrel vault has continuous thrust along its walls, it has difficulties in having opening on the sides.

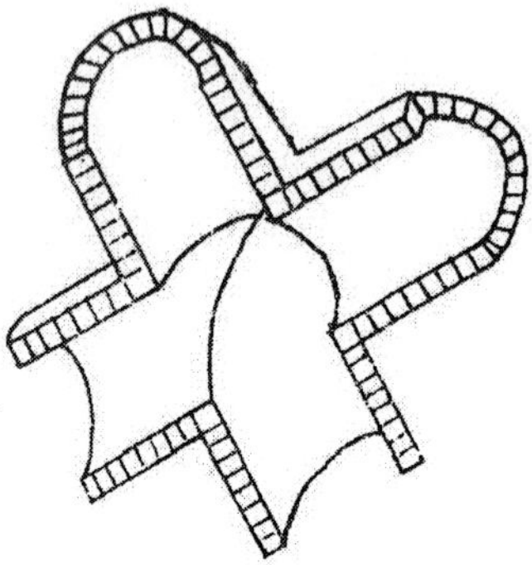

The Cross Vaults of the same span generate typical junction detail. It creates a square base with side Groins and the cross Groins.

When this intersection of two vaults is articulated as a structural system, it was known as THE GROINED VAULT.

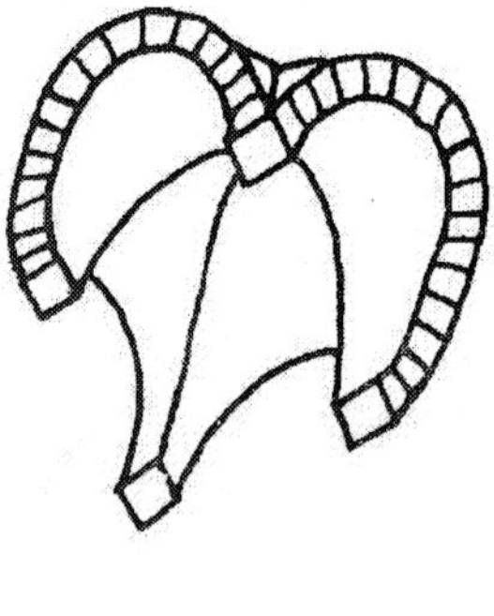

In the Square base vaulting, two dimensions of the GROIND ARCHES are to negotiate, the sides and the diagonals of a circle converging to its centre. The wedged stone from the crown of the larger dimension at the bottom does

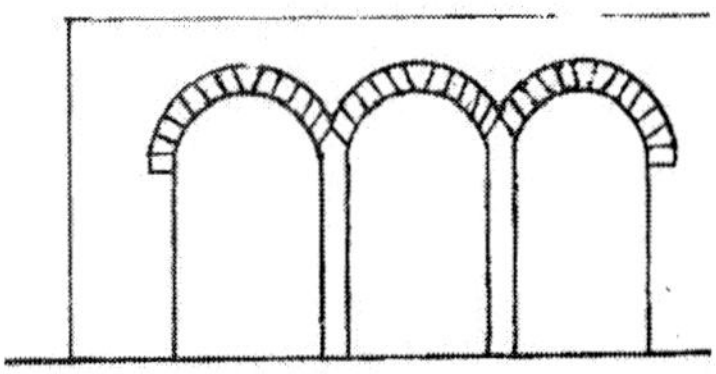

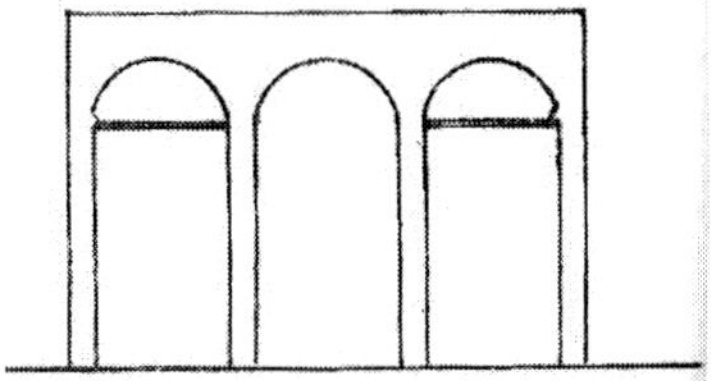

not smaller dimension at the bottom does not let it slip down and holds it in position AS LONG AS the base at the two ends of span do not give way due to ends of span do not give way due to the oblique THRUST or push due to the loading over the arch.

When in a series, the two adjacent arches neutralize their thrust into a vertical force.

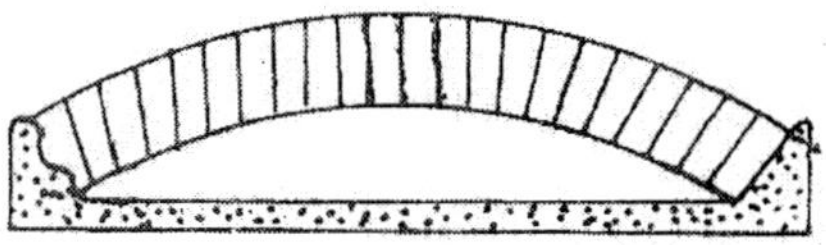

The thrust of an arch at its base can also be held by iron or steel bar. This is a Bow action. The outward push of the arch action is held back but the TIA BAR. Thereby, the thrust is neutralized to vertical gravity fore for the end arch. In this way, the end wall need not be solid to take the thrust if the tiebot is used.

The Visual Expressions of Architects

The language of arch action is expressed vividly in various periods by different architects.

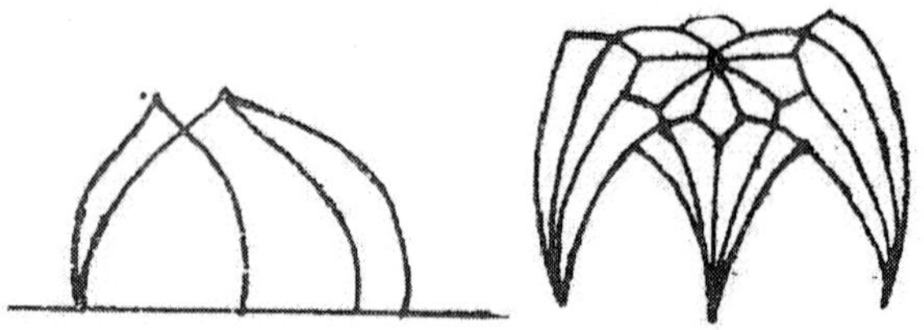

Expressing the key stone and the arch base for their importance and for a rectangular base, three dimensions of the different sizes have to be negotiated.

The early arches and vaults during the Roman period were semicircle. The crown of these groined arches did not meet at a point. Construction of vaults had complex curvatures. The groin arches of larger spans had to be flattened by making them into three-point or five-point arches. (Renaissance period)

Two-point arches or pointed arches were developed later during the Gothic period to solve this problem. Meeting of the crowns of different sizes of arches was made easy. The horizontal thrust component is also reduced to the minimum in the pointed arch construction.

Some of the most beautiful churches of the Gothic period exploited the groins or the ribs of the vault in making multiple rib vaults in fan shapes.

The Gothic Multiple Rib Piers and Columns

The FAN VAULTING SYSTEM of the ceiling had complex stress patterns. These, when transferred to the columns, and piers, developed very interesting and visually dynamic forms of the supports.

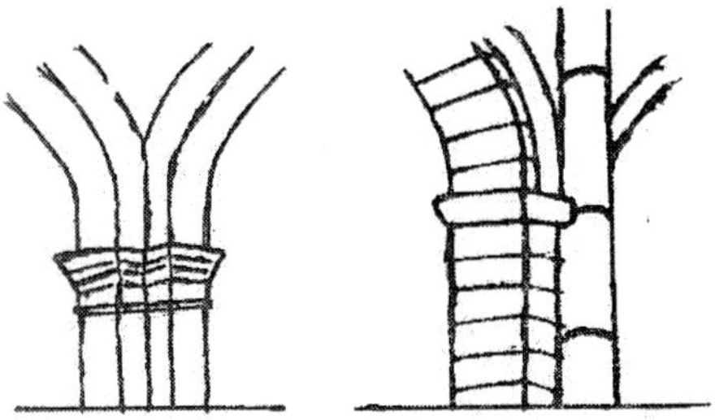

The Vaulted Domes

When the vertical rib system was rotated along the circumference of a circular base, it developed an interesting domical form. These domes were difficult to construct.

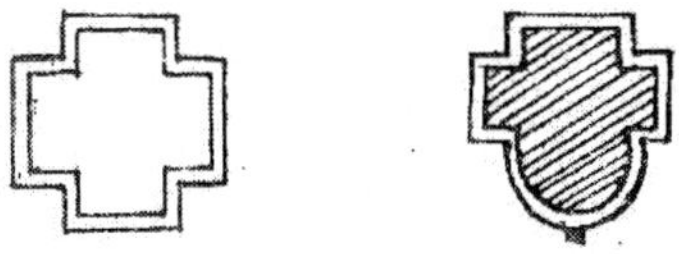

As they developed tremendous THRUST on the circular drum base on which these were erected. The domes of the Pantheon, Paris or St. Paul, London have triple shell domes to reduce and neutralize the Thrust. The base drum was even tied by heavy iron chains so as to keep it secure against the Thrust.

Buttresses

The buttresses are the supporting elements which resist the thrust form the vaults.

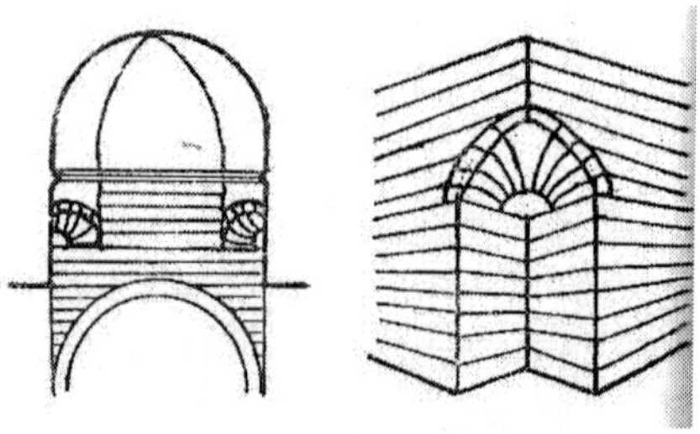

Flying Buttresses are buttresses which are spread more horizontally when the thrust forces are of higher order. Semi-Arch forms are created when the Fly of the buttress is too spread.

The Stalactites, the Pendentives and the Squinches.

The square base of the room is transformed to octagonal to round form to take the dome with the help of the above systems.

Stalactites belong to corbelling system. The other two are the Vaulting Systems.

8

Applied Vastu Shastra, the Vedic Architecture

It is in the wake of the Indian culture that the early conventions on Indian architecture emerged. At the advent of the Gupta age, several important earlier works such as Kautilya's Arthashastra and the Matsya Purana had incorporated chapters on architecture in a summary form. By the end of the period, the art of building had entered a renewed course of creativity by any different schools of architectural thought. Despite their diverse geographical locales, different structures were based on definite underlying principles with a distinct visual language. These principles are a part of the Vastushastra (the science of building).

The vast body of Sanskrit references on architecture is voluminous and scattered all over India. These texts deal with the whole gamut of building science, comment and proportion, astrology and ceremonies associated with the construction of buildings. The Matsya Purana gives a list of eighteen legendary preceptors who are referred to as instructors in the science of architecture. The most important figure among them is Vishvakarma, the expert Shilpi of the Gods, who engaged himself in building palaces. The next in importance is Maya, the architect of the demons. Of the innumerable texts, the Mansara and Mayamata originate from Dravidian Indian and represent the Southern School of Architecture.

These texts, as others, provide a religious validation for construction of buildings and were looked upon as a received body of sacred knowledge transmitted through the Guru-Shishya parampara. They were memorized orally, in parts, to give practical guidance to the priest-architect and his team of helpers.

The Gupta Empire made corresponding changes in the field of architecture. Two major styles of the Hindu temple, the Dravida (southern) and Nagara (northern) made their appearance. It is also worth mentioning that architecture itself was 'concrete' transmutation of Brahmanical percepts and had absorbed many current scientific disciplines-Vidyas-within its fold. Mathematics, geometry, philosophy, geology, astrology, divination, geomancy, semantics of form, myths and narratives formed an integral unit in the art and craft of buildings.

The transmission of this knowledge had to take a corresponding form and integrate all the sciences as one seamless discipline. It is for this reason that the Sthapati or Vastushipli, the priest-architect, had to undergo a process of integrated learning. To this day, the sthapaties take recourse to the collective knowledge of related discipline as to give shape to their creations.

The ethos of traditional architecture was rooted in Brahmanical ideas which had already found their articulation in the earliest religious texts of India by the end of the Gupta age. Traditional architecture was solely concerned with architectural meaning and its material translation into stone and wooed.

According to Hindu concept, the cosmos is a manifestation of a transcendent, no-dual, yet imminent principle, which unfolds the world and inhabits it as its animating principle. The one, undivided principle is known variously as Brahman or Purusha or Cosmic Being. This principle, which contains the universe in its womb in potential form, is the beginning of all spatial dimension and temporal duration. As it evolves, the original wholeness is split asunder, gets differentiated and gives rise to form a pair of opposites: the elements (earth, water, fire, air and space), and the world of the senses. The sacred cosmos emanates as a perfect Mandala. Whatever lies outside the periphery symbolizes the zone of chaos and anti-life. Whatsoever lies within the sacred cosmos reflects an integral unity of all existence

The sacred plan of the Hindu temple, its potent centre, inner spaces and the exterior composed of smaller shrines or shrine-images portray the indivisible law of creation as expounded in the Brahmanical writings.

The smaller shrine or shine images grouped around the centre are finite forms split from the all containing unity of the centre as fleeting transformations of the inner sanctum (Garbhagriha). They pulsate into the cardinal directions and disappear into the outermost boundaries. Space and time get located in the pattern of inter- relation between the built complexes.

The most potent architectural mechanism that embodied these 'cosmic' or cosmogonic principles is the Vastupurusha Mandala. A nuclear diagram of ritual significance, the Mandala provided a blueprint for building. It is more appropriate to refer to it as a linear computation that governs the rhythm, design, orientation and structural synthesis of a building. Its sacredness and special significance is stressed in all texts. all Hindu architecture is planned and regulated by it.

The Vastupurusha Mandala is a grid of square, regarded as a perfect figure, is conceived to be a fundamental form in architecture and all other shapes are derived from it. The square is oriented to the four cardinal directions: makes space comprehensible, and, therefore, it is looked upon as an all-encompassing symbol of the world. Tradition prescribes 32 types of the Mandala. The simplest one is a square. It is called Sakala (Diag.1) or one which has no parts and is prescribed for an ascetic's seat. It was a simple enclosure around the sacred fire and was never used as a site for building. The next one called Pechaka (Diag.2) contains four squares presided over by demonic powers. It was meant for the worship of Shiva in his terrifying form. The third type of Mandala which has nine squares, is known as Pitha or throne. All the rest are expanded versions of square to form a grid pattern of squares. Thus, the resultant figures are composed of 16, 25, 36, 49, 64, 81, and so c n, up to 1,024 squares. The construction of these diagrams follows a gnomic progression, a method known to the Greeks. The Mandala is dedicated (as its name suggests) to the building site or vastu. The earth is the primal vastu, since it forms a natural support to buildings. On its far spreading body, the site is marked out; that, too, is known as vastu.

In India, religious and artistic continuities survive. The theme of depicting the universe as a cosmic Purusha is used as telling metaphor to describe creation. The universe of the Hindus is portrayed as a colossal Purusha as the Mandala whose microcosmic body contains the world. The bounds of this anthropomorphized being constitute the regions of earthly and cosmic space.

The Rig-Veda states:-

- The man has a thousand heads, a thousand eyes, and a thousand feet. He pervaded the earth on all sides and extended beyond it as far as ten fingers.
- It is the Man who is all this, whatever has been and whatever is to be. He is the ruler of immortality, when he grows beyond everything through food.

- The man is yet more than this. All creatures are a quarter of him; three-quarters are what is immortal in heaven.
- With three-quarters, the Man rose upwards, and one quarter of him still remains here. From this, he spread out in all directions.

The universe is created and put in order through the dismemberment of the primeval male who is the victim of Vedic sacrifice. The imagery of dismemberment is linked to the creation of explicit elements.

Thus:

- The Moon was born from his mind; from his eye, the Sun was born. Indra and Agni came from his mouth, and from his vital breath, the Wind was born.
- From his navel, the middle realm of space arose; from his head, the sky evolved. From his two feet came the earth, and the quarters of the sky from his ear. Thus, they set the worlds in order. (Rig. Veda 10.90. 1-4-13, 14.).
- The ancient vision of the cosmos-man equation, scriptures on astrology describe the figures of Kaal Purusha (Diag. 3), or Time personified as an anthropomorphic being in whose body the stars and lunar asterisms are collectively represented. The theme of Purusha is carried through in the celebrated text of the Bhagavadgita (Chap.11). Arjun asks Krishna to reveal himself and there rakes place a vision of the all-pervading cosmic form of Purusha, "endowed with countless eyes and numberless mouths and innumerable centered in one." Virat Roop.

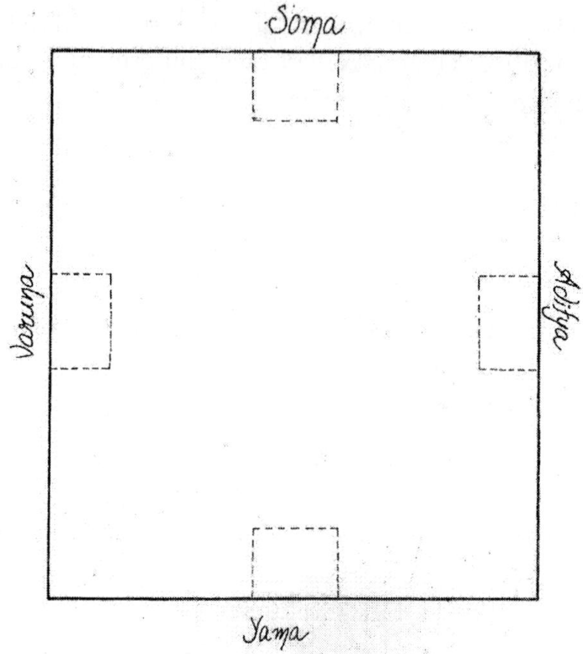

SAKALA MANDALA

Diag. 1

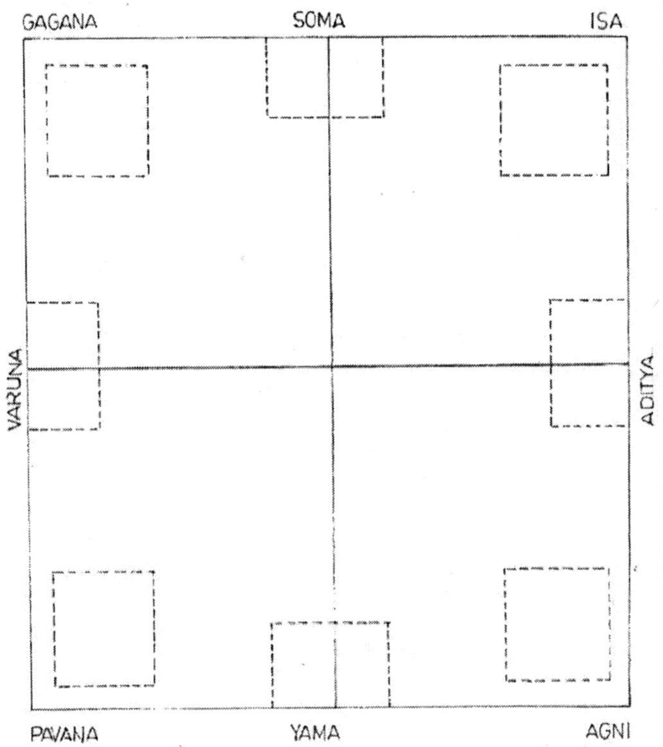

PECHAKA MANDALA

Diag. 2

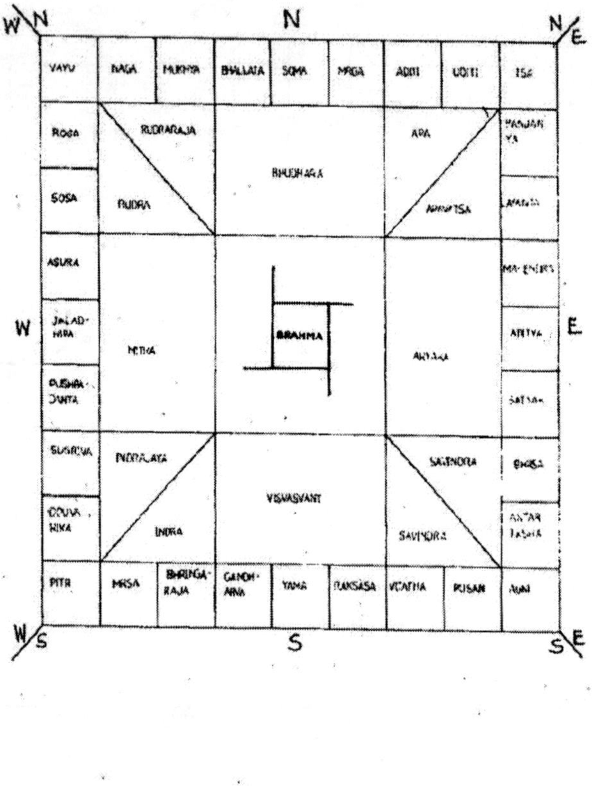

PARAMASHAYIKA
THE VASTUPURUSHA MANDALA OF 81 SQ.

Diag. 5

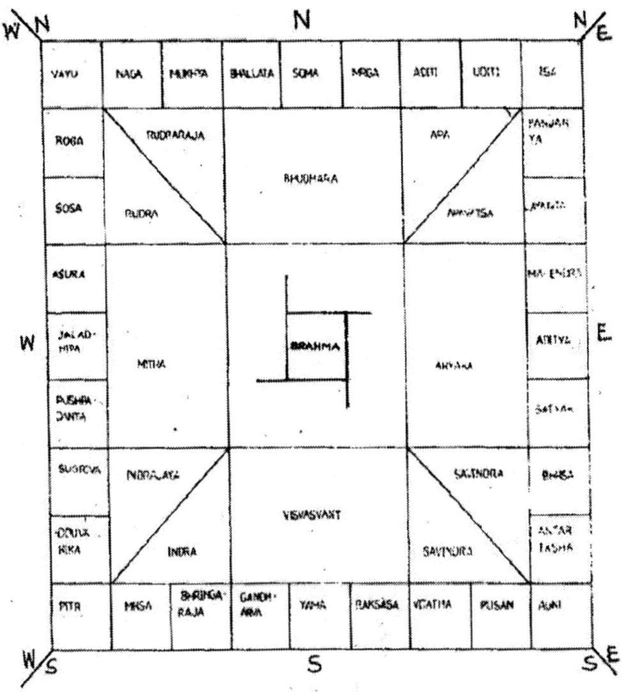

PARAMASHAYIKA
THE VASTUPURUSHA MANDALA OF 81 SQ.

Diag. 5

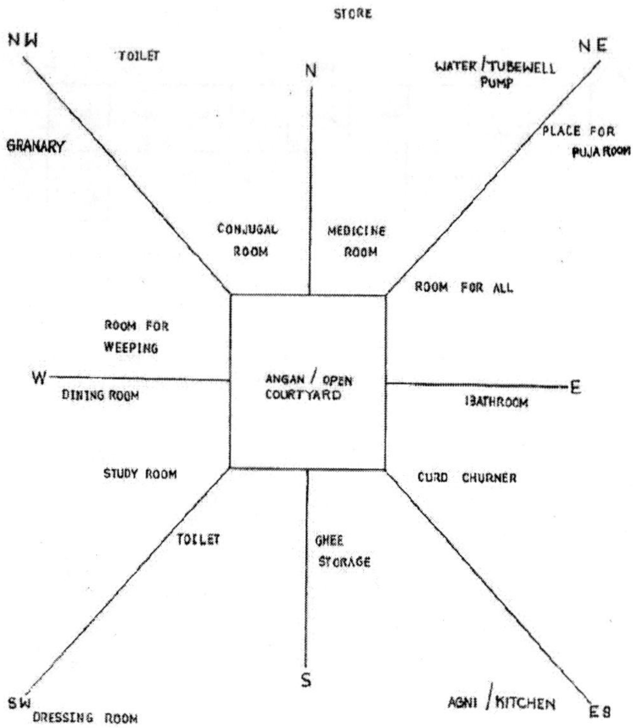

DIRECTION DIAGRAM ACCORDING TO VASTURATNAKARA

Diag. 6

VASTU-DEVATA MANDALA

Diag. 7

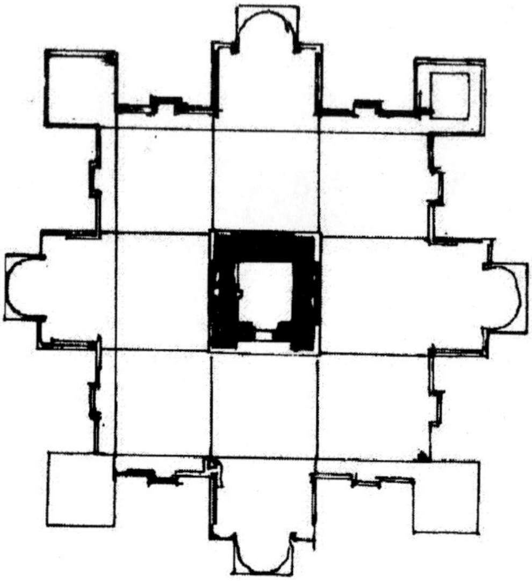

PAVANA	SOMA	ISA
VARUNA	PRITHVI	ADITYA
GAGANA	YAMA	AGNI

PLAN OF THE VISHNU TEMPLE AT DEOGARH

Diag. 8

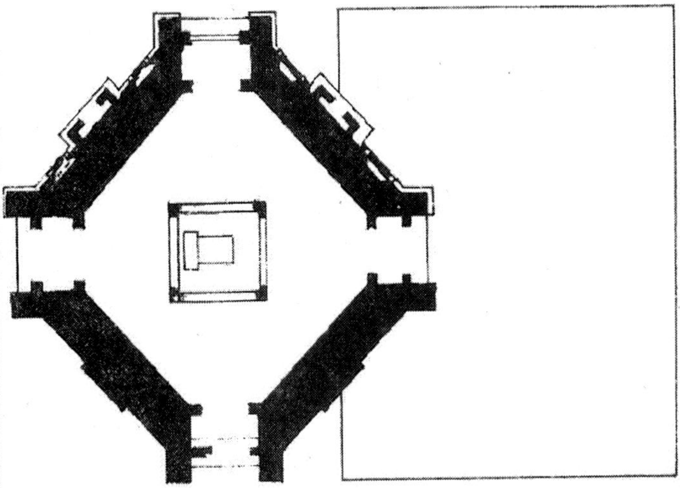

PLAN OF MUNDESHWARI TEMPLE

Diag. 9

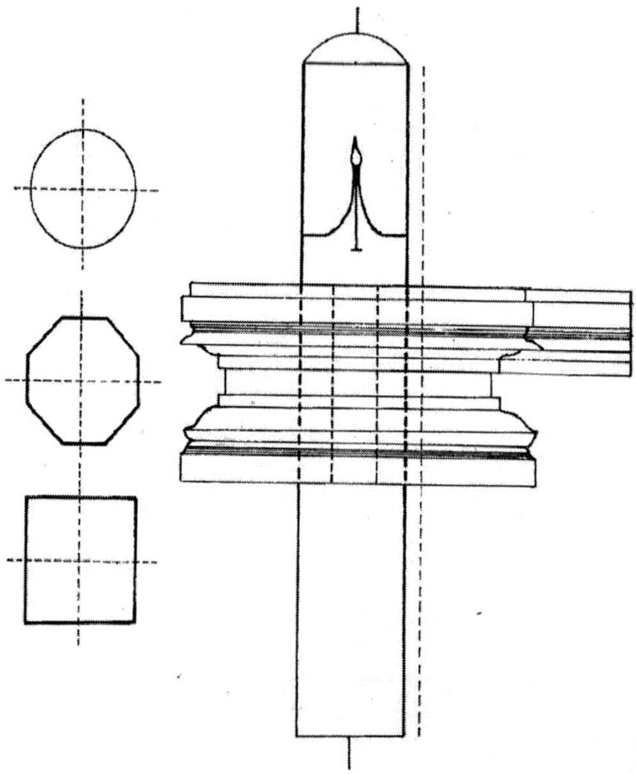

LINGA NALA AND YONI PITHA

Diag. 10

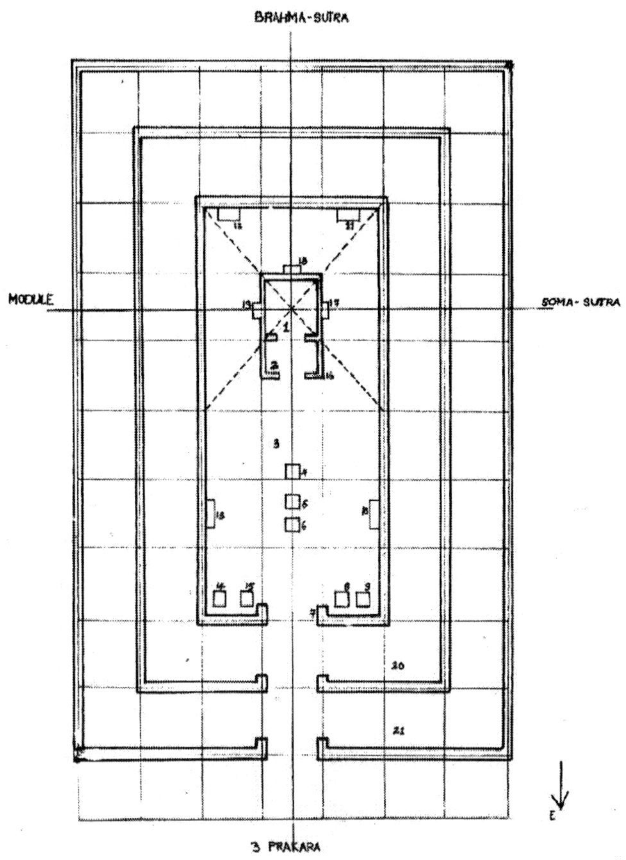

1. GARBHAGRIHA
2. MUKHAMUNDAPA
3. MAHA MANDAPA
4. NANDI
5. BALI PITHA
6. DWAJASTHAMBHA
7. GOPURAM
8. SURYA
9. SHANKARA
10. NAVAGRIHA
11. SUBRAMANYA
12. VINAYAKA
13. SAPTA KANYA
14. MADAPPALLI
15. CHANDRA
16. DURGA
17. BRAHMA
18. VISHNU
19. DAKSHINAMURTHY
20. SECOND PRAKARA
21. THIRD PRAKARA

N

PRAKARA BIJAM

Diag. 11

The Indian architecture has absorbed the theme of cosmic man in the conception of the Vastupurusha Mandala. Several legends from the Puranas describe the descent of the Purusha into the earth-bound Mandala.

In the square frame of these Mandalas, the square in the centre is presided over by the Supreme Principle deity. Encircling it are a number of smaller squares called Padas, or seats presided over by lesser deities who form a hierarchy. Around it in the border of the Mandala (of 64 Padas) are 32 divinities that preside over solstitial and equinoctial points. The eight cardinal directions are presided over by the eight planets. In this way, the Mandala symbolically represents an image of sacred space and symbolic movement of time measured by the day, month, year and wider cycles of the eclipses. With these affinities, this Mandala embodies an all-inclusive, contained image of the ordered cosmos. The boundaries of the site define the consecrated area, qualitatively distinct from the immediate environs. The building which the Mandala generates grows organically, similar to the microcosmos (Diag. Nos. 4 & 5).

The most important application of the Vastupurusha Mandala lay in the ritual of Pada Vinyasa or division of the ground-plan into a uniform grid. For this purpose, the Mandala is traced on the ground by making keep marks. The very process of drawing prepares the mind of the Vastushilpi to determine the relative proportion of the different parts of the building. The most exclusive area laid out on the 'site-Mandala' is the invisible centre, the residence of Brahma.

What the heart is to the body, this centre is to the meeting point of all centrifugal and centripetal energies of the land. It appears in monumental sacred architecture as an invisible vertical column, rising from the ground and reaching out to the highest point of the pinnacle. In the Hindu sacred architecture, this centre corresponds to the inner sanctum of the temple. In residential buildings, such as the Nair tharawads of Kerala, the centre is reflected in the open courtyard. Since the centre of the building is the embodiment of the incipient one, it is identified with Prana, the dynamic and vital life-force, invisible to the eye. Owing to these analogies, the centre is left bare; open the sky, wind and the elements. This is a free zone, the unmanifest energy source allowing for the natural flow of air and light. The open space of the central courtyard allows for controlling the excesses of climate. It is the genius of this tradition to have combined lofty symbolism with practical insight.

The Vastupurusha Mandala offered the formula to determine the functions of the building in relation to its orientation. The Vasturatnakara (Diag. No. 6) assigns specific functions to each direction. The south-east, for example, is dedicated to the element fire, presided over by Agni, and the north east to the element water. Invariably, the correspondence with the elements would determine the position of the rooms in the house. The space assigned t the region of fire, for instance, would be used for building a kitchen or reserved as a source for heat and warmth. On the other hand, water reservoirs, wells and bathing places would be erected in the north-east. The Mandala also served as a guide to locating the building on site and determining the position of the shrines in a temple complex.

Points where lines intersect are to be avoided for raising pillars and lintels. These points define physical boundaries. Open spaces were reserved for building all openings, windows or doors are to be constructed between the intersection. Once again, the formal graph lends itself to an uncomplicated design solution.

After the completion of the building, the Vastupurusha Mandala functions as an iconic construct – a device for adoration. It is held that the spirits of the site who occupy various squares of the Mandala need to be pacified and gratified by means of ritual offerings. For this grand celebration, every constituent of the structure is looked upon with great reverence and feeling. Doors and columns are decked with wreaths and ritual cloths, the house is decorated with leafed arches, and pitchers filled with holy water. The chequered-board pattern of the Mandala is traced on a Vedi (Diag. No. 7), a raised altar, and colored with powder. Oblations and offerings are made to all the deities one by one to the rhythmic chant of mantras, meant to disperse the malignant forces form the building and make way for positive powers to enter. The color made out of vegetable & flower.

It has been suggested that the Gupta period Vishnu temple at Deogarh is possibly the earliest surviving monument based on the Vastupurusha Mandala (Diag. No. 8). The temple is laid out in the innermost square of a nine-square Mandala, one of the most elementary forms of the Vastupurusha Mandala. A more recent example of the adaptation of the Mandala comes from Jaipur. The builders of Jaipur did not conform to any of the plans prescribed for towns by the Vastu texts. However, the layout of the city does conform precisely to the pitha or throne Mandala which the texts prescribe for general use. The pitha diagram has nine sub-divisions and is comparable to the earliest plans for Jaipur. The minor differences between the two plans have been explained by the emergencies of the site. The Manduka Mandala (Diag. No. 4) is composed of 64 squares. This Mandala was applied in varying flexibility and put to several creative uses. An example is the Shiva temple at Mundeshvari (Diag. No. 9), Shahabad District, and Bihar (7th century). The temple is based on an octagonal plan with four gates that open out to the four cardinal directions. The sanctum is also given an octagonal shape.

The basic geometry of the equilateral octagon was first applied to the temple according to the principle of Vedic mathematics. The 64 Pada Mandala was then accommodated to the octagonal plan of the temple. The Paramasayika Mandala of 81 divisions (Diag. NO. 7) is also of considerable importance. These two (Manduka and Paramasayika) distinctive Mandalas were commonly used in temple architecture. The Sthandila of 49 squares and the Padmangarbha with triple enclosure described in the Southern texts seem to have been more faithful to the prescription. They lie at the root of several Southern temples.

In the design of creation, the cosmic and microcosmic man and nature unite in a single thread. Applied architecture created formulae to accommodate this vision of unity between man, nature and the built environment. Tradition prescribes that the site on which the building must be raised must be situated amidst trees, groves, water courses and lakes. Even the indigenous system of soil testing had to take into account the sprawling landscape, tree cluster, shrubs, water bodies. Elevations and depressions and the shape of the site. The astrologers and Sthapati identified the site by examining the soil with regard to its consistency, color, odour, taste and tough. The elevation of site, the vegetation in the environment, and the water resources in the vicinity were carefully studied.

According to the Grihyasutras, the quality of the soil is then examined in two ways: A pit is dug and refilled again with the earth taken from it. If the cavity is not filled up by it, the soil is to be rejected. If the cavity is filled up but is even, the soil is said to be of medium quality; if there is excess of earth after filling it, the soil is considered to be of excellent quality. The next process is to fill the site with water at sunset, and leave it overnight. If, the next morning, there is water in it, the ground is said to be of excellent quality; if it is moist, it is of middle quality; if it is dry, it is to be rejected. After the soil is tested, the mason fashions a peg (Shanku) from a sacred tree, and nails it to the ground. Directly above it, the foundation is established.

Architecture is sanctified in the embrace of nature. It is a fundamental principle of traditional architecture that nature is not to be destroyed but controlled. The built structures are meant to harmonize with the natural surroundings. They must yield to the environment with the same rhythm as trees and plants bursting with buds and blossoms yield to the ever-flowing force of gravity.

Kautilya's Arthashastra (Chap. 2, p. 466) prescribes the maximum use of the environment and gives an impressive list of natural forts- an island in the middle of a river, a rocky tract or a cave, thick forests, stretches of deserted land devoid of water. These natural sites as possibility should be considered before building. One of the first stone temples in Mahabalipuram (7th-8th century AD) uses land and seascape to its maximum advantage by placing half the temple in the land and half in the sea. Similarly, a cluster of trees is never mindlessly razed to the ground but used as a focal point of the building. This principle has been universally acknowledged and applied throughout in traditional complexes and vernacular architecture. It helped greatly to preserve the ecology of the area.

Thus, architecture was largely shaped by natural resources of the locality where the building came up. Hence, the geographical and geological aspects, while being preserved, influenced building styles and choice of material. The trap and granites of the Deccan, for instance, produced a large number of caves. The alluvial soil of the Indus and lower Ganga favoured terracotta and brick; the volcanic potstone of Halebid and the light colored setelite which was quarried in the vicinity of Rajasthan and North India helped the growth of respective styles.

Tradition had also recognized the multi-fold blessing of the plant world. Very often, the efficient use of plants is made as a preventive measure. For example, when wooden posts are to be installed, in order to save them from fire, aquatic plants, the sipala (a water plant), are grown around them to keep them moist. Trees were a natural link between the subterranean stratum and the earth, and between the earth and the heavens above. They empowered blessings of fertility, abundance and curative prowess. It is for this reason that the nomenclature of trees finds a place of importance in Vastuvidya. The manuals give a classification of trees and prescribe their placement around a building. Trees, such as the banyan, peepal and the drumstick should not be grown near the house as they have fine roots that waken the ground. Trees and shrubs that invite insects, snakes and owls are not recommended. Trees with the hard inner core may be planted near a home, but those with a hard outer ring may be placed at a distance outside the compound. Whatever species they belong to, tress that are felled for wood for building are treated with live and sympathy as though imbued with a spiritual force akin to man.

Thus, the Sthapati, who wishes to search for wood, goes to the forest at an auspicious hour.

Behind the Shilpi community of craftsmen (Sthapatis, temple designers and sculptors lies a tradition of scientific and philosophical knowledge. elaborated here is their system of training which meticulously follows the ancient Shastras, combining technology, philosophy, self-awareness and, above all, Bhakti (devotion to the Divine) to create the masterpieces that form part of our tradition and heritage.

Among the many Parampara (hereditary) traditions of India, the tradition of the Vishwakarma is unique. The modality of transference of knowledge, as practiced by this community, is both oral and practical, and builds up a holistic universe of thought and understanding. The rigour and discipline required in creating objects which would defy time and last beyond the life span of each generation of artists has imbued this tradition with tremendous resilience and sensitivity. It is this that has enabled them to maintain the purity of their identity and skills without falling prey to seduction of wealth and material acquisition. Unfortunately, very little is known about the Shilpi (one of the five groups in the community) and the texts that they followed, though some mention has been made of the builders and designers of some of the great temples: Kevada Perunthachan of Mamallapuram, Kunjaramallan Rajaraja Perunthachan of the Tanjavur Temple, and Parameshwara Perunthahcan of Utteramerur.

The community claims descent form artists and craftsmen mentioned in the Vedas and the Puranas which identify five separate groups based on particular skills and training.

- Manu – The blacksmith, also known as the Karmakara – makers of weapons as well as metal tools for agriculture and sculpture;
- Mava – The wood craftsman or carpenter, also known as Rathakara, made rathas, furniture and also wooden images and abhishekha ladles for temple use. They were also the ship builders;
- Twashta – The maker of the beautifully designed copper, bell-metal vessels that can be seen in many parts of the county even today.
- Shilpi – The temple designer and sculptor today marginalized into craftsmen. They were the designers of the entire built environment as well as the executors of all types of buildings. Using vegetables colors.
- Viswagya – The jeweler or goldsmith, also known as the Swarankara.

The common name for all Vishwakarma group is the Shilpi. The Manasara speaks of four Shilpis who came from Brahma: Vishwabhu, Vishwavidh, Vihswastha and Vishwasristhta. The next generation comprised Vishwakarma, Maya,

Twashta, and Manu. From these four descended Sthapati, Sutragrahi, Vardhagi and Tashaka. Today, Sthapati is used as a title or suffix by practicing individuals of the community. Though Vishwakarma is the general community name, they are known locally as the Panchalas in the Punjab, Kammalar in Tamilnadu and Tachan in Kerala. In addition to being artists, they have also been scholars in the Vedas and are also known as Acharyas.

The Principles

The Vaigyanic (scientific) base to the Shilpi's creativity can be classified under major concepts:

Vastu and Vaastu

The world "Vastu" is taken to mean the ultimate particle in the microcosmic universe or and (egg) as well as the subtlest particle in the microcosm. It is believed that this Vastu is the origin of creativity in both the universes, existing as it does as the infinite unchanging particle. Brahma or primal energy is an integral part of this particle. The Vastu Shilpa Shastras state that this primal energy exists in three states, namely:

- Nishkala (part-less), Aruvam or amorphous. An example is the concept of the linga;
- Sakala or Vuruvam or morphic. An example is Vishnu or Chandrasekhar Murthy;
- Sakala Nishkala or Aruvuruvam or morpho-amorphic. An example is the Mukha Linga.

The Linga

The Jyoti Linga is concept of the luminous shaft of creative energy which is perceived as the universal centre, as also the luminous thread of the Atma. The traditional believes that the amorphous being is like a whirlpool of light, at the very centre of which lies the tranquil core, a cylinder of luminosity. This is also called the Brahma Nala (Diag. No. 10).

Vishnu

The spirit of energy of the earth is called Vastupurusha, and the shilpaic tradition speaks of this as the form of Rangaraja or Shayana Vishnu. In the Bhoomi Pooja, this energy is invoked to give the desired benefits so as to make man's life on earth peaceful. Since Vishnu stands for the spirit of the earth, most of the images of Vishnu are made of earth mortar or Katu Sarkara. There are two systems of belief in Vaishnavism – Pancharatna and Vaikhanasa. Vishnu is also seen as the epitome of the amorphous energy, and the morphic image placed in the sanctum is perceived as direct representation of the Divine One.

Prakara Beejam

In the temple complex, ht position of the Garbhagriha is considered the most important. This position is seen as the Moola Sthana of the complex. Taking this as the basic unit, the rest of the complex is laid out as multiples of the module. Hence, if the Garbhagriha is taken as X, then the Prakara will be 1 X on either side of the sanctum, and in front there is projections of the module up to 3X which forms the mukhayam of the temple. In this rectangular form, the Garbhagriha is like a seed that constantly expands outwards to form the 1,3,5,7 Prakaras (Diag. No. 11).

Technology

To transfer the Vigyana (science) onto an observable plane, the Shilpi makes use of a numerical system, both for sculpture and architecture. Primarily, the Shilpi creates an image for worship. He also designs and executes the environment for housing the divine image as well as for the residence of human beings. The first is known as Devalaya and the second as Manushyalaya.

Tools and Measures

In the stone Shilpi's yard, the tools are made of mild steel and are sharpened and forged in the furnace in the year itself. Form the coal used in the furnace, the marking pencils are made. The kavi required for the final markings and for defining of the sculptural plumb lines is made from red powder obtained from the soil by sieving and drying it. The standard scale is made of teak wood, but other subjective scales are also prepared for the measurement of the tala and the projections from the central axis. For this, mature bamboo is used.

The tools for cutting, shaping, polishing and carving come in a variety of shapes and sizes. There are five different types of measuring rods adopted by the Shilpi for various categories:

- Survey of land, village, town, roads, building sites
- Residential buildings, forts, palaces, temples, tanks and wells
- Beds, swings, seats, chairs, tables and other articles of furniture
- Temple cars, carts, chariots and palanquins
- Idols, icons and images

Units of Measurement

8 Paramanu = 1 therthugal (chariot dust)

8 therthugal = 1 immi (diameter of human hair)

8 immi = 1 ellu (sesame seed)

8 ellu = 1 nell (paddy grain)

8 nell =1 viral or angula (finger length)

The viral is equivalent to 13/8". 24 such viral form a hasta or muzha which is the standard measuring rod (24* 13/8" = 39" or 3'3").

The hasta or muzhakol is a very important element in the Shipli's world, and the giving of the muzhakol forms an important part of his coming of age. The rhythmic complexity of a particular temple or complex can be unlocked if the basic muzha can be identified. In fact, the major temple towns have created a muzha of their own based on the specific rod employed for the setting out of their dimensions, such as the Tanjai (Tanjavur) muzha (24 angula or 2' 9"); muzha (25 angula or 2'10 3/8").

Vedic Architecture Order

The skill and training of the Shilpi is, thus, directed towards the creation of the tangible form for the Divine Being and to housing it in a space that would reflect the Universal Reality. In this tradition, sculpture and architecture are not separated but part of a total divine experience. The primary sculpture or shilpa is the form of the Nataraja which expresses the endless creativity of primary energy. The primary architecture is the Garbhagriha, a cube that encloses the primary energy. Thus, architecture becomes that enclosure which is capable of enclosing vibrant energy, and sculpture is the representation of this energy in morphic form.

Where architecture is concerned, the orders maintained through the adoption of a modular planning technique called Pada Vinyasa or Pathi Manam. The land is divided into grids with sutras running north-south and east-west. The primary east-west axis that runs through the centre of a Vastu is called the Brahma Sutra and the north-south as Soma Sutra.

The plot may be divided into even or odd number of padas. The central points are called the Brahma Sthana, the outer rings as Brahma Pada, and pechaka Pada.

This order is carried out in the case of both individual buildings as well as in the layouts of villages and towns. In the case of temple layouts of villages and towns, the module is divided into smaller units so as to facilitate the adoption of rhythmic modules in the horizontal and vertical planes in the wall or in the projection of the basement (Adishtana). In the vertical plane, it would be the height of the pilaster or the height of the basement. Multiples of these measurements are used at every level so that the overall effect is very much like the rendering of a rage in all its complexity, while the percussion instrument maintains the tala in the background.

The deities, too, have their particular positions in this order. The Shaivite tradition, for example, gives positions to the images in a complex arrangement of 400 padas. In the Vaishnavite tradition, the image of Vishnu is positioned in the Daivika or Manushya Pada. This arrangement has been adhered to very faithfully in Tamilnadu and some other parts of the South. Images of Buddha and the Jain Thirthankarans are placed against the wall at the rear of the Garbhagriha.

To be able to achieve rhythm and order in the entire Vedic architectural and sculptural piece, the Shilpi uses the above principles in an extremely simple manner. The rhythm gives rise to a visual order and structural rigour. The understanding of materials gives rise to marvels such as the musical pillar and the ball in the lion's mouth. The perfection of joint and finish comes from a disciplined work ethic and community ethos. Flashes of genius and evocative beauty grow out of strict adherence to a social belief and the adoption of a grammar of design.

9

Hindu Architecture in Vedic Period Influenced by Vastu Shastra

Indus Valley Architecture (Harappa and Mohen-jo-daro) (3250 to 2750 B.C)

The Indus Valley people had made building of various size which were plain and solid rather than beautiful and color decorative. They had constructed three types of buildings-dwelling houses, shrines or public halls and public baths. Dwelling houses are many in number. While the smallest have no more than two rooms, the largest are so vast as to appear almost as palaces. That most of these houses were double-storeyed is quite clear from the marks of stairways leading to the upper stored. They were made of baked bricks and mud-mortar. Sometimes, when strength was required, lime and gypsum-mortar was also used. The houses were furnished with paved floors and were provided with doors and windows. The roofs were made of mud, reed and wood. It is especially noteworthy that almost every house had its own well, bathrooms, courtyards, drains and kitchens.

There were public building also. One of them was a high-pillared hall, 80 feet square, which was perhaps used as an assembly hall to transact the business of the state. Another such structure was a state a granary, about 200 feet by 50 feet, which was further sub-divided into smaller storage blocks for storing different types of grains. But the most important was the Great Bath (at Mohen-jo-daro). The actual bathing pool was about 39 feet in length, 23 feet in breadth and 9 feet deep. It was suggested that this bath was used by the general public on certain religious festivals. The pool was provided by galleries and rooms on all sides and perhaps also with a 'Hammam'. It had a flight of steps at either end and was fed by a well nearby. Every attempt was made to make it strong and water-tight. Many thick layers of well-baked bricks laid in gypsum-mortar were joined together for the purpose of making the whole construction very strong.

Many statues and figurines, both of animals and men, have been found. Among these statues, those of a young bull, a strong watch-dog, a shawl-wearing yogi dancing girl with her hand on her hip and a dancer standing on his right leg while raising his left leg in front, are worthy of note. All these statues faithfully display bodily features and look quite life-like and realistic.

Buddhist Architecture in India (Early Mauryan Dynasty) (400 B.B)

Mauryan Dynasty was the first dynasty which established a single stable government in North India. This resulted in a marked cultural progress with achievements in the building art which gained the royal patronage. The evolution of Aryans, nomadic ways to urban ways of life gave birth to a new enlightened class of merchants, artists and europeds. In this materially progressive group residing in the towns and cities, the Vedic religion as instituted by the Brahmins was of a rather mechanical and a lifeless character. This feeling led to the growth of religious and philosophical speculations, and in the environment of speculations and enquiry, Prince Siddharth Gautama discovered a new meaning of life and religion. The religious orientation directed by adopted by millions of followers, and this new religion was named as Buddhism.

Vardhman like Gautam found his own path of salvation. His vision led to the founding of another major Indian religion, i.e., Jainism. To Vardhman, the Mahavira, the concept of God and the abstruse teachings of Brahmins were of no value. The aim of life is eternal bliss which is possible by purification of the soul and could be achieved by living a balanced monastic life, of which non-violence was touchstone. However, the Buddhist and the Janis preaching of non-violence had little effect on the contemporary temporal style.

Rulers continued to battle for control of strategically territories. Mauryan dynasty was the first dynasty which established a stable single Government in Northern India. The Mauryan King Chandragupta following the advice of his counselor, Chanakya, had chosen to press towards the Indus region.

Alexander, Porus and Chandragupta

Persians retained control over the trans-Indus region, until their own Empire crumbled under Greek pressure. After winning the battle of Marathan, Alexander's army appeared in the Indus Valley in India. He crossed the five rivers ad reached the banks of Beas, from where he was forced to return back as his army was tired. In the process, he left behind a floating Greek population under a power vacuum. In the entire region, Chandragupta Maurya filled the Vacuum. Thus, for the first time in the Indian history, the plains of the two great rivers Indus and Ganga came under a single great ruler, Chandragupta Maurya.

The Mauryan Dynasty of Patliputra

The modern capital city of Patliputra stretched for miles along the Ganga, being only one and half miles deep. The King's palace was a grand version of the rectangular huts of the humble villages. A series of barrel vaulted timber roofs supported over rows of stone columns instead of brick walls. The columns were drafted depicting scenes of Buddha's life. According to Magasthenes, the famous Greek envoy of the capital city of Mauryas, the King's palace was set within beautiful parks starred with lakes, fountains, sprayers, swings and artificial hillocks. The entire complex as protected by a timber reinforced wall. The city itself was a cluster of houses of varying plans, invariably supported with barrel shaped roofs water proofed with tiles or thatched. The sculptured frieze of Buddhist stone carvers depict horse shoe shaped windows and lattice screened balconies overlooking the street.

In the suburbs where the large houses of the well-to-do were built around open court and surrounded by private gardens, large public gardens seem to have been laid out for the recreational purpose. The modern concept of the garden city by Abenzon Hourert is inspired by the planning of the capital city of the Mauryan, Patliputra. Ashoka the Great inherited the Mauryan Empire and continued the ambitious policy of expansion. After winning the kingdom of Kalinga, which was an event of great historical significance, Ashoka determined to set up an enlightened Government, and also, in due course of time, he became the moral leader of the whole civilized world. Ashoka adopted Buddhism and started propagating the message of Ahimsa.

STUPA AT SANCHI

Diag. 1

The Monument Principles of the Ancients

The finest and the most compact geometrical forms, a square and a circle were the two options opened to the Buddhist architects to select as a shape of their building plans, they selected circle, the shape without an edge which symbolized the Buddhist wheel of law. The shape of the buildings, the hemispherical shape was designed on the most fundamental restriction, the Broad Base, tapering at the narrow apex.

Wood was the common building material during the age of the Buddha and it was only sometime later stone began to be used with some frequency , slowly replacing the early use of perishable wood, first perhaps for the construction of royal residences and city walls. The remnants of the stone rubble ramparts of Rajgriha, the early capital of the Mauryas during the 4th century B.C., represent perhaps the earliest use of stone known today.

The Buddhist Stupa

The embryo of the most powerful architectural forms of the Buddhist Stupa emerged for the first time under the architectural patronage of Ashoka. The total form of the Stupa, the plan, elevation and section were derived from the circle. Earliest stupas were constructed in brick with mud mortar, but, to ensure the lasting effect of Buddhism, Ashoka chose stone as construction material.

Sanchi: Stupa at Sanchi

The death of Ashoka resulted in the return of the Vedic religion and the Buddhist monks began to retire from the centre of urban power. They, however, continued to enjoy the patronage of the wealthy and sophisticated mercantile class. Founds continued to pour in to help the Buddhist monks to build their new monasteries in more peaceful and solitary environment. The largest and most famous of these blossomed upon a hill top in Sanchi. In the Ashoka period, a semi-circular brick mound, some 70 feet in diameter, had been built here. The Stupa was enlarged to double its size by building another stone faced mound increasing the diameter of the original to 120 feet and its height to 54 feet. Sixteen feet high from the ground level of the Stupa, the builders created an elevated Pradakshina path perhaps reserved for the clergy, the traditional one at the ground level being open to the common pilgrims. The Great Stupa at Sanchi is a hemispherical dome with its top truncated and crowned by a triple umbrella, standing upright at the centre of a masonry pedestal and surrounded by a square railing.

The crown of the hemispherical mound was flattened out at the top to make place for a circular platform, form the middle of which rose a three tiered stone umbrella set inside a square enclosure, marked out by a low stone fence.

In the process of carrying out the enlargement of the Stupa, the traditional timber fence surrounding the original Stupa had to be pulled down. It was replaced by massive and austere railing, fabricated entirely out of stone. The construction of the fence in stone was the first experiment in the use of stone as semi-constructive material. Octagonal stone pillars, 18 inches in diameter and 9 feet high, were planted along a circular periphery at a distance of about 2 feet from each other. The space between each pillar was spanned by three numbers of 2 feet deep lens-shaped horizontals, which were meticulously tenoned into corresponding mortices, cut in the pillars. The railing was tapped by a massive stone coping giving it a total height of 11 feet.

Toranas

The work on the extensions and refurbishing of the Stupa went on for almost 100 years. The imagination, religious zeal and vigour of the builder as well as the coffers of the mercantile patronage, however, seemed inexhaustible. The wondrous pathway around a Stupa was like a forbidding wall from outside. A touch of invitation was lacking. Toranas were introduced as the gateways to match the magnificence of the Vedika. Elaborating once again on traditional village forms, the rural bamboo gateway of the Aryan village was transformed by the Buddhist builders into a great 34' high Torana. Four such gateways were installed at cardinal points of the railing. The techniques of the stone masonry employed in constructing the Toranas was, no doubt, as primitive as those in erecting the railing. Nevertheless, after erecting the stone uprights, the stone masons realized the futility of cutting mortices and making tenons in stone. Instead, for the first time, he applied the rationale of building with stone and merely spanned 20 feet between the verticals with curved stone beams resting firm and square and sailing over either side of the uprights.

Vihara

The Stupa led to the growth of other ancillaries. Buildings were needed to house the resident monks. In contrast to the richly sculptured gateway of the Stupas, the paced of residence in their bareness, reflected rather the inherent austerity of monastic life. These were built as a series of individual cells or dormitories enclosing rectangular or square open-to-sky court. The open court served all the community facilities at places, including a well for drinking water. The cells, on the other hand, afforded the monks sufficient privacy for the practice of meditation. It is evident that the basic idea was only an enlargement of the traditional concept of the "house around a courtyard". In due course, these came to be known to be known as Viharas.

The Stambhas

Inscriptions were carved on the columns of stone instead of mere slabs, and these were set up at regular intervals along the roads leading to places of Buddhist pilgrimage. Columns measuring 40 feet in length and weighing about 50 tons were carved out from a single block of sandstone. These massive pillars were then carried, unbroken and intact to sights over 100s of miles away. The tapering of shaft of the column once it reached its destination was varnished and polished to give it a unique mirror-like luster. It was a fantastic achievement with sedimentary rock-like sandstone. The columns, sometimes, rose straight from ground without any base like the trunk of tree or at some places had circular brick platform at its base. At the top was mounted a large sculpture figure of an animal. One of these, the famous sculpture of the four lions, has acquired great popularity since being adopted as the National Emblem of our country. The sculpture executed in a style reminiscent of the Persian design weighing 5 tons and about 7 feet high was e3ffectively joined to the pillar by a 2 feet long cylindrical copper dowel tenoned accurately into the shaft and the sculpture without the use of any cementing material.

Chaitya Halls

The great Stupa, though a magnificent structure, had its limitations. It was essentially an open air edifice incapable of being used in bad weather. The need was felt, therefore, for an enclosed hall in which a miniature Stupa could be constructed, and people could conveniently worship the year round. A rectangular hall with a semi-circular wall behind the Stupa was adapted as a shape of the Chaitya Halls to give physical identity to their philosophy.

The roof of such a structure was the barrel vault in timber, covered with tile and supported on brick walls framed by Timber pillars. The entire 3 composition was built on a high plinth enclosed by the railings.

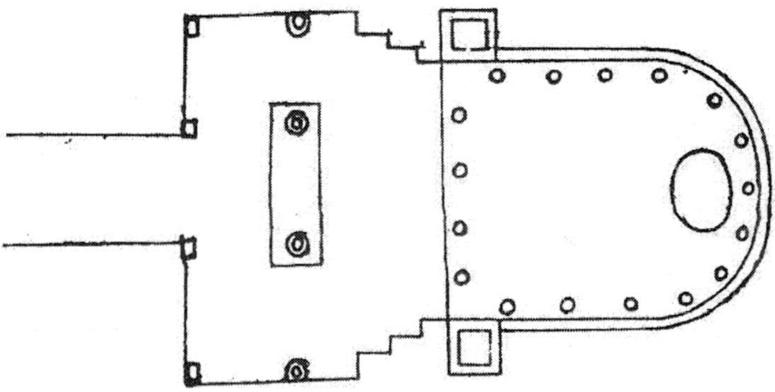

Marble Stupa in Amravati

Amravati Stupa was about 190 feet in outer circumference, and was the largest ever built in India. It was most profusely decorated, both architecturally and sculpturally.

The cardinal points of the upper Pradakshina path were marked out by clusters of free standing pillars or 'Aryakas' giving an unusual artistic distinction to it. While no Toranas have been erected, the entrances to the lower Pradakshina path are marked out by stambhas which were also planted at regular intervals along the path. The Stupa of Amravati was built in white marble and was a dazzling monument. Today, nothing remains except for the trench making its site. In planning the more important were given for the orientation on the principle of Vastu Shastra.

10

Temple Architecture were Planned on Vastu Shastra Rules?

The Hindu temple is where the God dwells, surrounded by his priests, ministers and attendants, and so the spot where the temple stands is holy ground, to be selected with due care and after deep consideration. According to the Vedas, there are certain places, the Tirthas or Kshetras, which are especially sacred and these sites are the most worthy for the worship of God.

The BRIHATSAMHITA tells that Gods prefer to live where there are rivers and springs, by mountains and in shady groves, and if in towns, surrounded by pleasant gardens full of flowers and natural beauty. Only such sites could be conducive to divine contemplation and spiritual harmony. And only in such places-by the river bank, the sides of lakes, on the quiet seashore, in arboured groves and gardens-should temples be built, whether large or small. However, certain ancient texts prescribe different sites, according to the deity enshrined.

The Sthapati or chief craftsman designed the temple on the orders of the Yajaman, the donor of the temple, supplying the necessary funds. It is said that he had to have a knowledge of architecture and building construction, that is, of the VASTU SHASTRAS, of astronomy and mathematics, even of other arts and crafts. He should have good judgement, an intuitive feeling for design and planning, the ability to put all his knowledge into sound practice. Of course, the Sthapati did not work alone. He was assisted in his labours by other Shilpis like surveyors, builders, masons, sculptors, stone-carvers, all supervised by the chief craftsman. The one wishing to build a temple had, thus, first to find a good Sthapati well-versed in the Shilpla Shastras and possessing practical craft knowledge and experience, as enjoined by the ancient books.

The old Vastu texts are equally precise about the actual constructional principles of a temple. A foundation platform consisting of stone blocks was first made on the ground with a few steps leading into it. On this plinth, the walls were built, usually made up of slabs of stone laid on without any binding cement or mortar, but cohering on the principle of balance and equipoise. The walls had to support the weight of the tower, if any. The cellar housing the divine image was usually kept small and covered with stone slabs forming a false ceiling in one single span. However, the span of the much larger Mandapa had to be reduced by the construction of piers of pillars, few or many as necessary, connected to one another by means of beams which also joined them to the inside walls. Stone slabs rested on the pillars and the beams to form a ceiling for the Mandapa.

An ancient manuscript which says that wood or stone are worthy of kings, priests, Brahmins, and even hermits, but unsuitable for Vasishyas and Shudras-the merchant and labouring classes, respectively. This makes one believe that the building material to be used was, in some way or other, related to the caste system. However, many other ancient manuals on the science of architecture and building principles allow the use of stone for all temples, whatever the ca of the donor or builder. But the color of the stone is nwo0 related to the caste. White stone alone was to be used by the Brahmins, red by the Kshatriyas (the warrior caste), yellow by the Vaishyas and black stone by the Shudras. This was especially applicable to domestic architecture. The same differentiation applied even if bricks were the material of construction. It is, however, doubtful if these strict injunctions could have been rigidly followed, or if it was even always possible to do so.

The plan of the temple site is the Vastupurusha Mandala, a gird generally divided into sixty-four or eight-one squares. This may cover the whole site or just the area to be occupied by the shrine itself. The Mandala is square and knowledge of this is enjoined on the builders, for it is on this, divine into padas that the temple will eventually stand.

In short, the Indian architecture, both secular and religious, is based on the grid plan, a plan made up of identical squares or padas, and squares divided by diagonals to form equilateral triangles. It is taught in the ancient Shastra that each square is the dwelling place of a deity, the central ones being the locus of the A Universal Brahman as symbolized by Brahma. And as the Hindu temple planning is based on religious interpretations, the architect was not free to deviate from the precepts laid down in the Vastu Shastras, hence, more or less uniformity of structure in any one place down the ages has been noticed, even if in various building materials and differing in the degree of complexity and elaboration at the site.

It is believed that the square reflects all existence in the Indian mind. It symbolizes the earth which itself is derived from the circle. But it also signifies the body of Purusha, the primeval Man, who also stands for the personified Cosmos. According to the Vastu Shastras, the Mandala can be drawn in thirty-two different ways. The unit is the single square, which may be further divided into four, nine sixteen, twenty-five, thirty-six, forty-nine, Sixty-four, eighty-one, and up to 1,024 smaller squares: the padas. The size of each individual square is immaterial. The squares determine the planning and placement of the main shrine, its adjuncts and subsidiary additions, and even the ratio existing between the thickness of the walls and the dimensions of the interior areas.

Two grids are considered the most important: the Manduka Mandala formed of sixty-four padas, and the Paramasayika Mandala consisting of eighty-one squares. However, many South Indian texts consider the Mandala of forty-nine padas also to be of great significance. The central axes of the plan are oriented in the direction of the cardinal points. According to Hindu thought, Brahma is surrounded by forty-four lesser Vedic Gods, four just round the Brahma-sthana (the locus of Brahma), eight in the next ring, and thirty-two in the outermost squares. Of these Vedic Gods, eight of those in the four corners and the middle points of each side are the guardians of the cardinal points and thus fix in space the orientation of the padas.

After deep thought and many calculations, the temple site is finally decided upon in the name of the divinity who will one day be installed therein. Rites precede the commencement f the building proper. The site is first cleared and cleansed and rid of the demons and evil spirits by prayers and propitiation. The goddess of the Earth is invoked by Puja (worship) to ever stand firm and steady under the sacred edifice to come. After this, the ground is levelled and the plan of the plan of the temple drawn on it. As mentioned before, although the Mandala is primarily square, it may be turned into triangles, hexagons, octagons or even circles by means of diagonals and other dividing lines. But the final form must evolve out of the square, for this is the essence of all Hindu architecture.

The job of the priest-architect or the Sthapati was, indeed, a difficult one. It was not enough for him to design a well-balanced, architecturally pleasing structure. He had to take care to see that the entire temple was in magical harmony not only with time and place, but also with the stars of the patron having the temple built.

Incomprehensible rules, as laid down in the Vastu Shastras, hedged him on sides. He was not free to play about with length, breadth and height of the different parts of the temple structure, for all had to conform to the basic requisites. There was the necessity for perfection, not necessarily absolute perfection. The ancient texts lay down the mathematical concept of imperfection, that is, not a whole number but one where a small fraction is left over on division. True, the architect used the integral part of the number, but considered the fractional or decimal part of the number to be of equal if not of greater importance. In the Indian architecture, the theory of proportion is the 'doctrine of the remainder'. The builder is more concerned with the remainder which has to conform to the 'rules of proportion'.

After the proportional values of the different parts of the temple were settled, further calculations had to be made relating to the caste of the donor and the time the temple was intended to last.

And, thus, from its initial square plan, step by step, year by year, the temple slowly pushes its way upwards-a memorial to the builder and a place of abiding glory for the enthroned deity. For, say the ancient Shilpa texts, having built the temple, such should be its glory and greatness that the priest-architect, the Sthapati, and the Shilpikar should themselves be struck dumb with awe and wonder at their own supreme creation for the ever-lasting glory of their God.

11

Proportion and Measurement for Vastu Shilpa and Vastu Kala

The text of the Vastu Shastra has been waiting for hundreds of years to be unearthed from manuscripts which are quite inaccessible without the guidance of a special dictionary that would also be instrumental in bringing to light many new things hitherto left unexplained in inscriptions and general literature.

All architectural terms used in Manasara, with explanations in English and illustrative quotations from cognate literature were available for the purpose in Manasara series.

In Vastu Shastra, architecture is taken in its broadest sense and implies what is built or constructed. Thus, in the first place, it denotes all sorts of buildings, religious, residential and military and their auxiliary members and component mouldings. Secondly, it implies town planning; laying out gardens; constructing market places; making roads, bridges, gates; digging wells, tanks, trenches, drains, sewers, moats; building enclosure walls, embankments, dams, railings, ghats; flights of steps for hills, ladders etc. thirdly, it denotes articles of house furniture, such as bedsteads, couches, tables, chairs, thrones, fans, wardrobes, clocks, baskets, conveyances, cages, nests, mills etc.

Vastu architecture also implies sculpture and deals with the making of phallic, idols of deities, statues of sages, images of animals and birds. It includes the making of garments and ornaments etc.

Vastu architecture is also concerned with such preliminary matters, as the selection of site, testing of soil, planning, designing, finding out cardinal points by means of gnomon, dialing; and astronomical and astrological calculations.

In this chapter, we discuss in brief about Pattern and Formation, Creation, Proportion and Measurement in regard to Vastu Shilpa and Vastu Kala.

In Vastu Shila there are two main branches:

- Deva Shilpa
- Manava Shiplpa

They call it Shilpa Shastra.

The Deva Shilpa

The Deva Shilpa is mainly used for the designing and construction of temples, Garbhha-Griha, pavilions and the detailing of ornamental design such as decoration pillars, beams, walls, jali etc. also, images of different Gods and Goddesses, deities and their ornaments.

The Manava Shilpa

The Manava Shilpa is mainly used for designing and construction of building, used for public utility such as Public Places, Public Buildings, Houses, Resting House (Dharamshala or Hotels) stables for horses, birds and their detailing of carvings in stone and din wood, on pillars beams, walls and furnishings. Refer Diagram No. 1a & 1b.

Proportion and Measurement in Vastu Shilpa and Vastu Kala

Deva Shilpa

- Temple
- Garbha Griha
- Pilles
- Images of Different Gods
- Deities
- Pavillion
- Ornaments

Manava Shilpa

- Places
- Building
- Houses
- Riding Animals
- Birds
- Carving (Stone and Wood)
- Furnishing

Vastupurusha Mandala (Yogini)

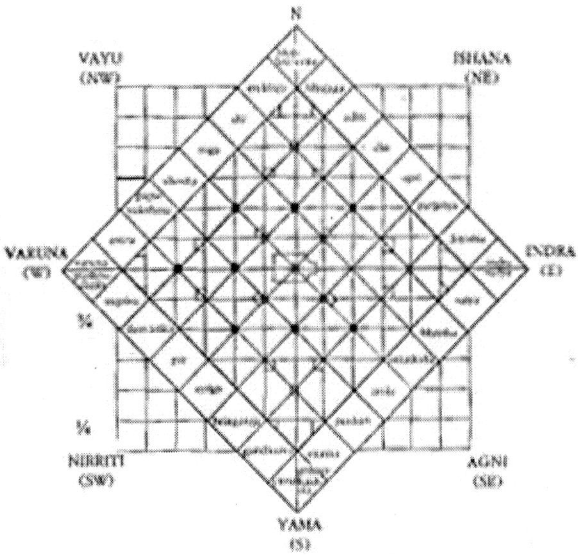

For Manava Shilpa and other Buildings
Diagram la

Brihat Samhita

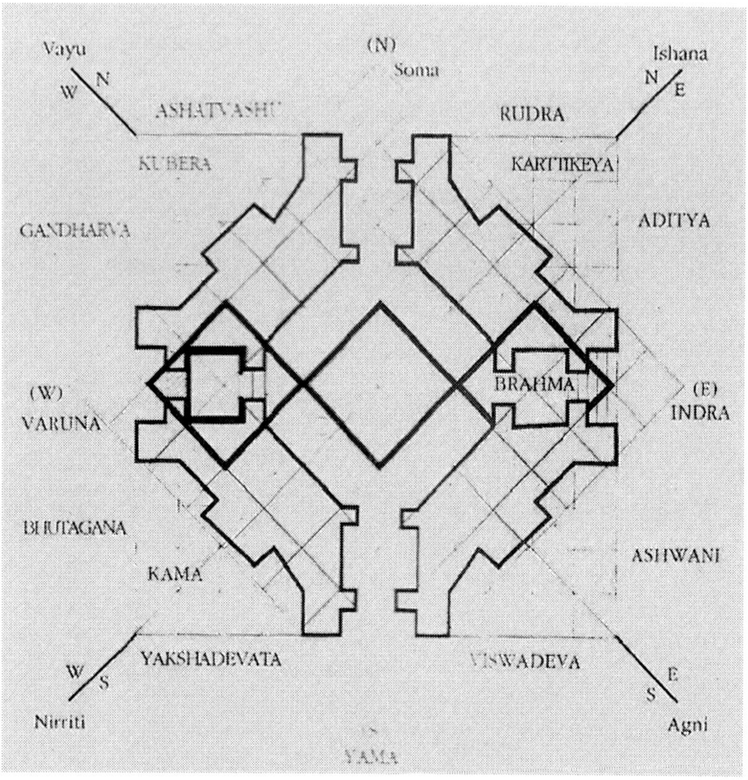

For Deva Shilpa (Temple Design)
Diagram 1b

In Shilpa Shastra, the artist who is responsible for design and carving the design has to be very accurate in measurements and has to be particular about proportion in relation to height, breadth and length and their carvings have to be perfect to the scale.

The system of measurement was so perfect that the smaller unit of scale was 1/8 the human hair and was called paramanu or the Atom as, explained below:

The System of Smallest Unit of Measurement in Shilpa Shastra was Paramanu or Atom:

8 Paramanu (Atom)	=	1 Hair End
8 Hair End	=	1 Nit
8 Nit	=	1 Louse
8 Louse	=	1 Barley Corn
8 Barley Corn	=	1 Aangula (Finger)
Angula the Finger Breadth	=	¾ Inches
12 Aangula	=	1 Span
2 Span or 24 Angulas	=	1 Hasta
4 Hastas	=	1 Dhanush (Bow) or Danda (Rod)

Tala: A Principle Unit of Sculptural Measure Equal to the Length of the Force or (Storey)

Proportion and Measurements of Temple building and Structure

The height of an image or structure or temple was determined and compared with its length and breadth. The same mainly of five proportions systems are highly technical and extremely minute in detail and are found in Manasara II page 124 and Vol. IV page 100 are:

- Santika (Height) = (breadth)
- Paushtika (Height) = ¼ of (breadth)
- Jayada (Height) = 1, ½ (breadth)
- Dhanda (Height) = 1, ¾ (breadth)
- Adhuta (Height) = twice (breadth)

That is:

Breadth – 12, 14, 16, 18, 20

Length – 13, 15, 17, 19, 21

Height – 22, 23, 24, 25, 26

In the case of large type building four-storeyed or more the dimension proportion is:

- Breadth – 11, 13, 15, 17 or 19

- Length – 12, 14, 16, 18 or 20
- Height – 21, 22, 23, 24, & 25

They have two different scales, as system of measurement was for Deva Shilpa particularly for Deities where they have larger scales, a bigger measurement than for the Manava Shilpa. Similarly, they reduce their scales for Goddesses than to ordinary human then to animals and to birds etc., as shown and explained in (Manasara IV ch. XI page No. 102) ***Vastu Kala***

Largest Type of Dasa Tala With Comparative illustrations of the other Nine Tala

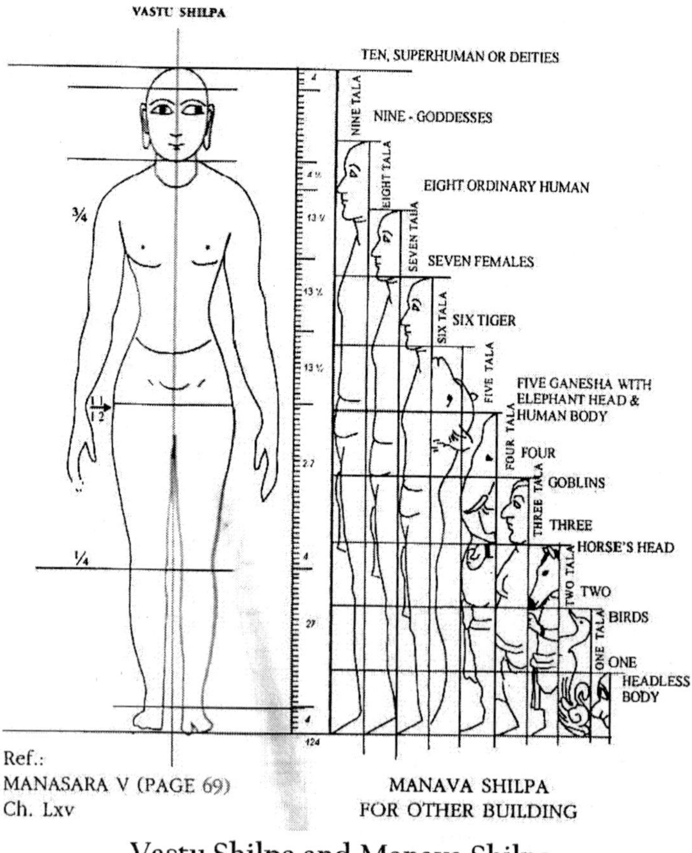

Ref.:
MANASARA V (PAGE 69)
Ch. Lxv

MANAVA SHILPA
FOR OTHER BUILDING

Vastu Shilpa and Manava Shilpa
Diagram 2

The most interesting thing to know is that they were also more particular about the size, shape, proportion of the body line particularly for the Superhuman, the Deities. They used Plumb Lines to draw out perpendicular and horizontal proportion of the Body Line as shown in Diagram No. 3 and 4.

Deva Shilpa Deities for Temple Designs

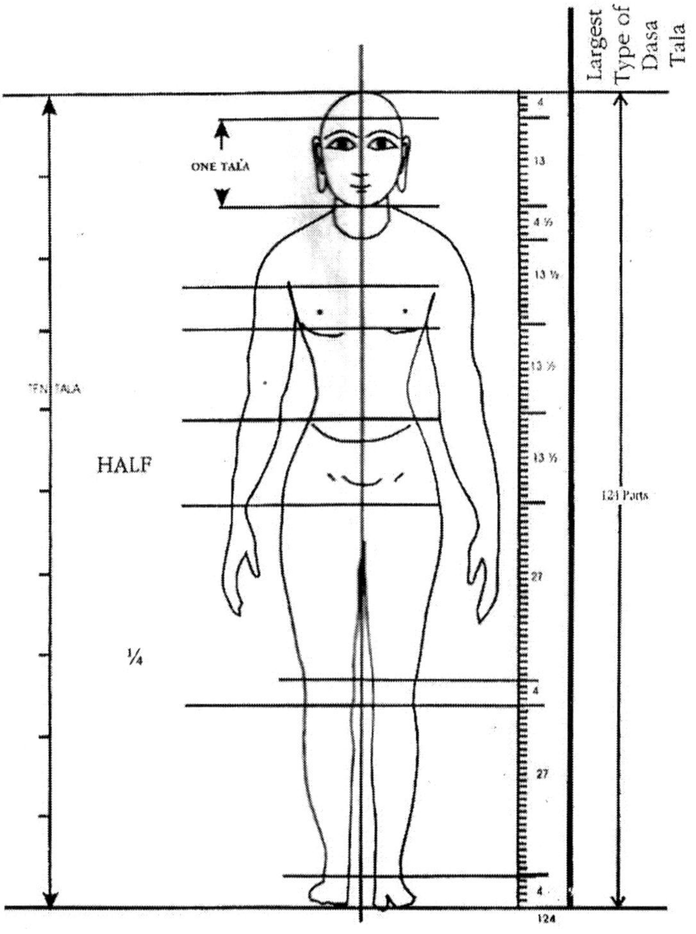

Largest Type of Dasa (Ten) Tala in this Measures of 124 Parts (Limbs) of the body. It is used for measuring Superhuman and Deities
Diagram 3

Plumb Lines Eleven to Find Out Perpendicular and Horizontal Measurements

Distance Measurement between Different Parts of the Body of an Image

Diagram 4

In Vastu Kala also a particular attention has been given for the proportion of body line as shown in Diagram No. 5.

Vastu Kala

Diagram 5

Temple Buildings

In Temple Buildings they used stone and timber of different types and quality for structure, column and beams. Similarly, they give much attention to the proportion in respect to the height, breadth and length as shown in Diagram No. 6.

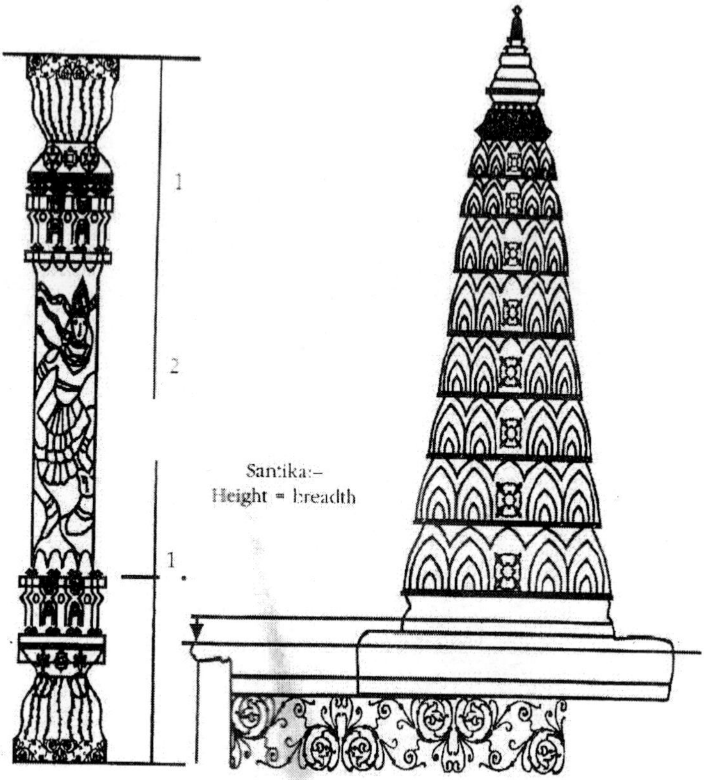

Proportion Measurement

Diagram 6

Structure and Column (Stambha)

The roof rest on the load bearing column called (stambhas or Kumbha) of different shape from square or circular to Octagonal, pentagonal and Hexagonal divided in four parts. The bottom part called pedestal, then Base, then Shaft and upper part. Refer Diagram 7.

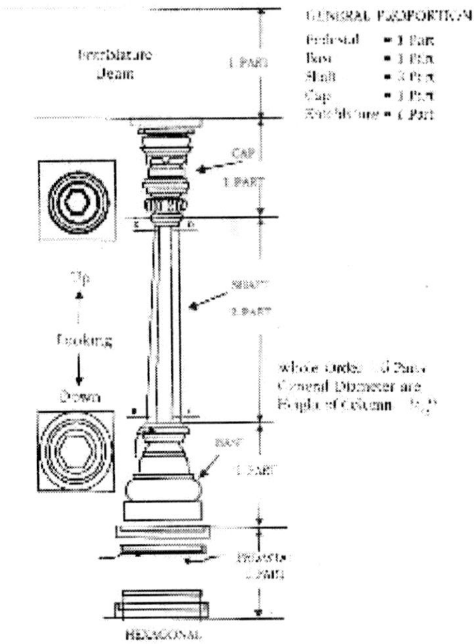

Column Kumbha - Stambha

Diagram 7

The detailed drawing of circular, square, Hexagon and Pentagonal Columns with beam (Entablature) and the supporting brackets are as shown in Diagram 8 and 9.

The Columns

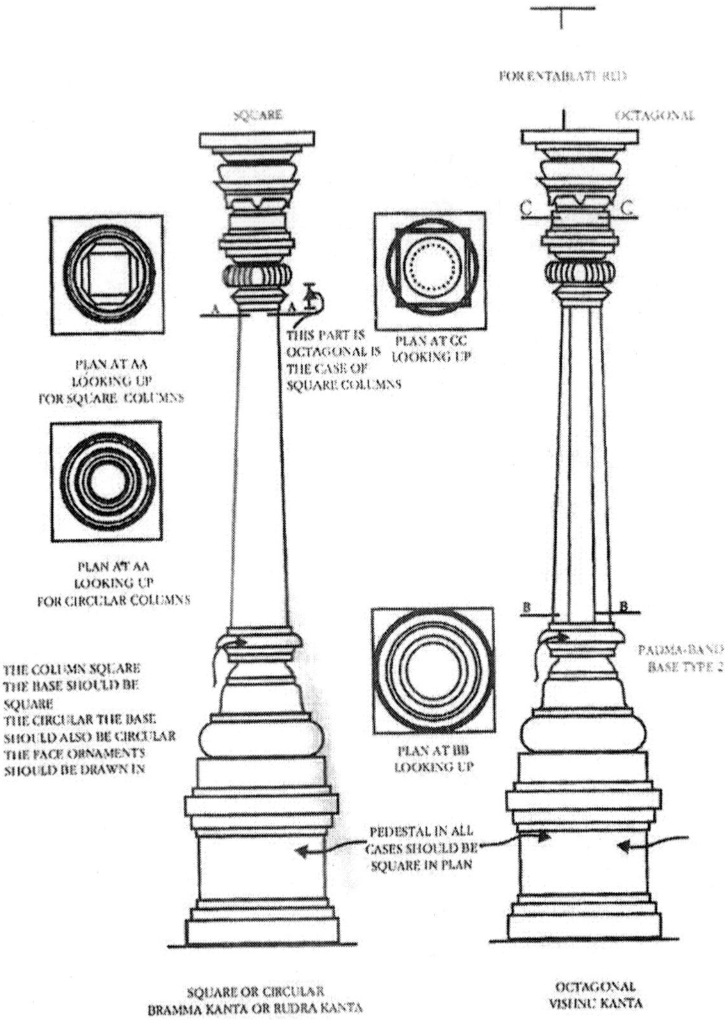

The Palika Stambha Class
Diagram 8

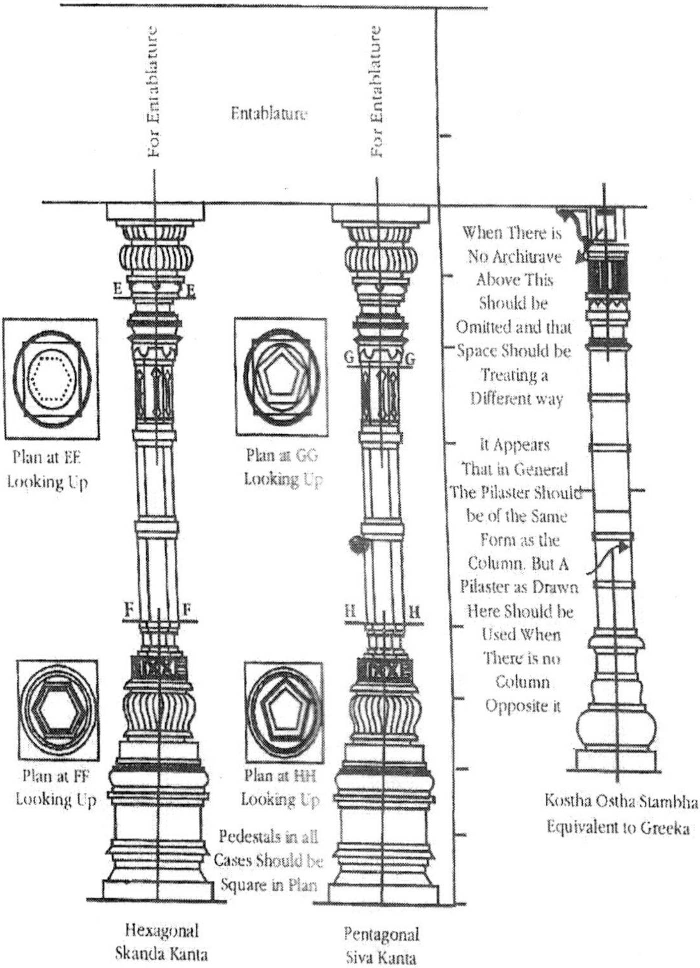

Hexagonal – Pentagonal Kumbha – Stambha
Diagram 9

Gates and Windows

They gave special attention in Vastu Shilpa and Vastu Kala Shastra for the position of Main Gate, its size and decoration according to the status of the owners Refer Diagram No. 10.

The gate-house and Window-Ch.xxxiii Windows for Temples, Kings, Brahmins, Vaishyas and Sudras.

Note:

The Windows openings have been divided into 4 rectangular units and the Jalis have mainly been designed on those units. The Window Walls for Temples and Placed May be of an elaborate creepers pattern also.

Windows for Vaishyas and Shudras

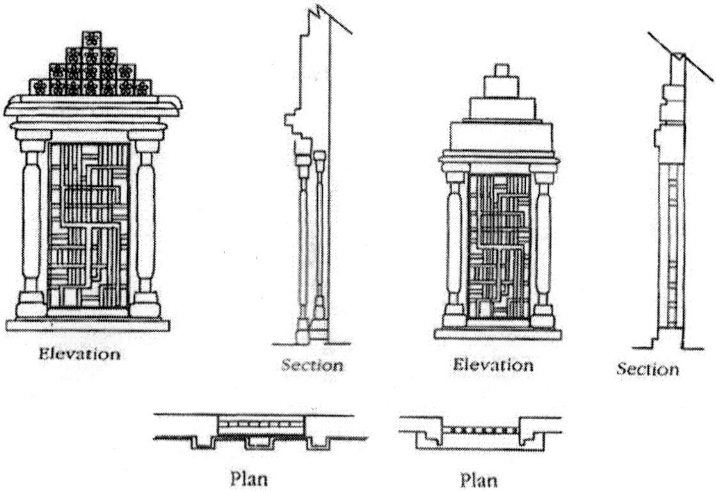

For Temples of Kings 'Kshatriyas' and Brahmins
Diagram 10

The other gates and window opening depend on the orientation of the building, the size of inner courtyard and numbers of storeys as described in Diagram No. 11 for single story building where windows and doors are on all the four sides.

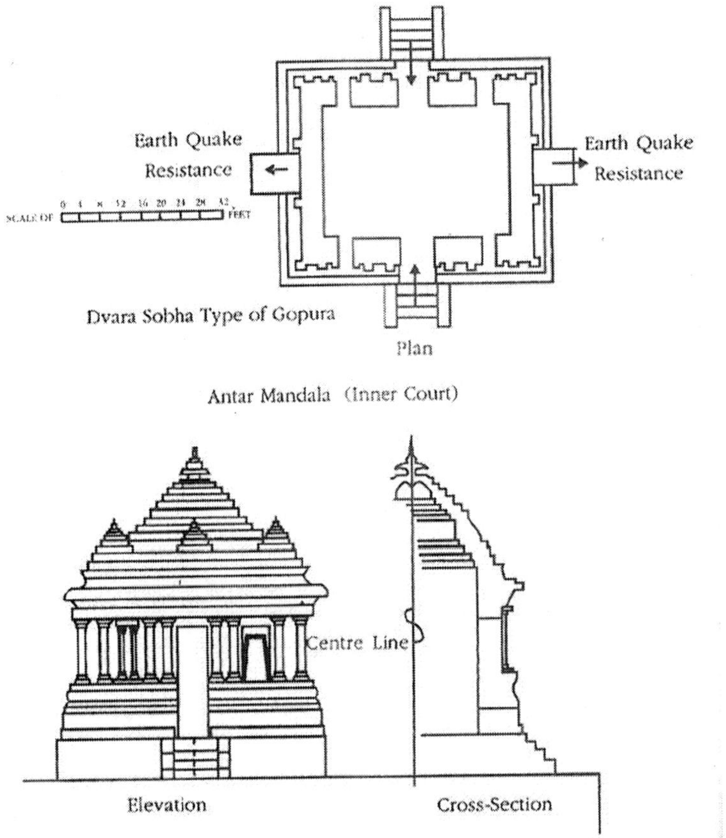

Dvara – Shobha (Beauty of the Gate) Single Storey for Temples & Residential

Diagram 11

In two-storey building, the first floor structure and load of structure have been taken on the extra column, taken from the inner courtyard Refer Diagram No. 12 and open from all sides.

Window and Gate for Two-Storeys

The Gate Houses and Windows—Dvar-Shala Type for the second Court

Length (In plan) = 1 Width

Height in Elevation = Width

Note:

These entire gate houses are both for Temples and Residential Buildings.

In residential building the Gopuras Should always be less in number of Storey's than the main edifice, but not so in Temple.

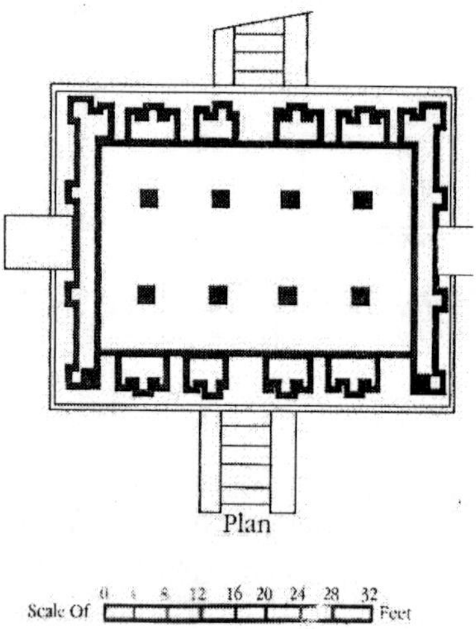

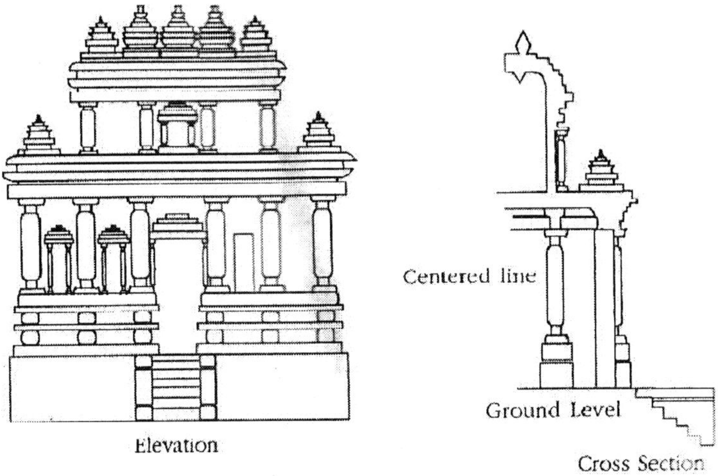

Dvara – Shala (Gate House) Antanihara (Second Court)
Earth Quake Resistance
Diagram 12

Similarly, in three-storey buildings, the first and second-storey are equal in size but smaller from ground floor. The load has been equally distributed in all four sides to balance the structure. Equal opening of windows has been provided Refer Diagram No. 13.

Window and Gate for Three-Storeys

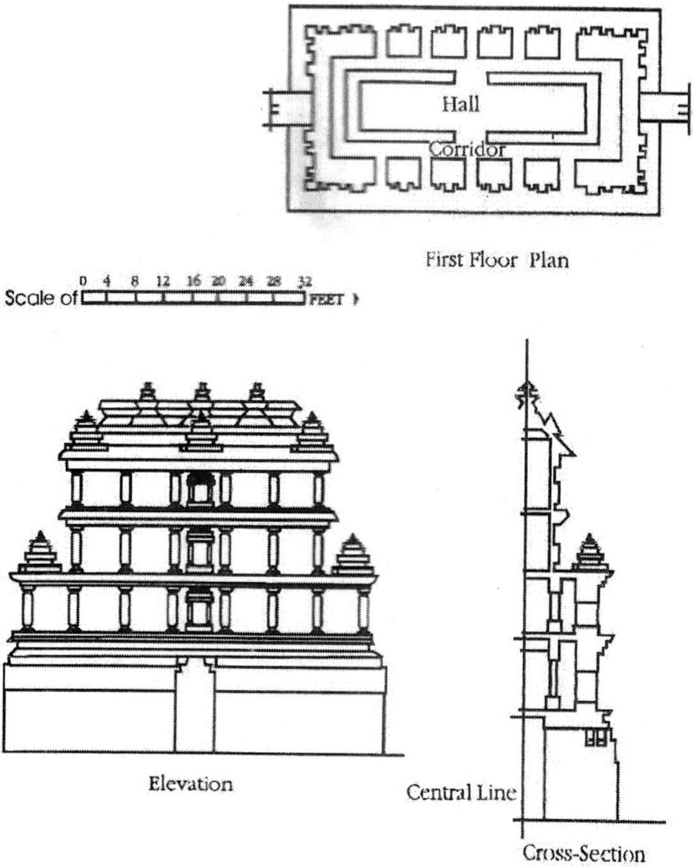

DVARA-PRASADA (Gate-Palace) (Third Court)

Earth Quake Resistance

Diagram 13

Four-storey buildings for temples or residence, the ground and first floor are equal in size as well as second floor and third floor are also equal in size Refer Diagram No. 14.

For Four-Storeys

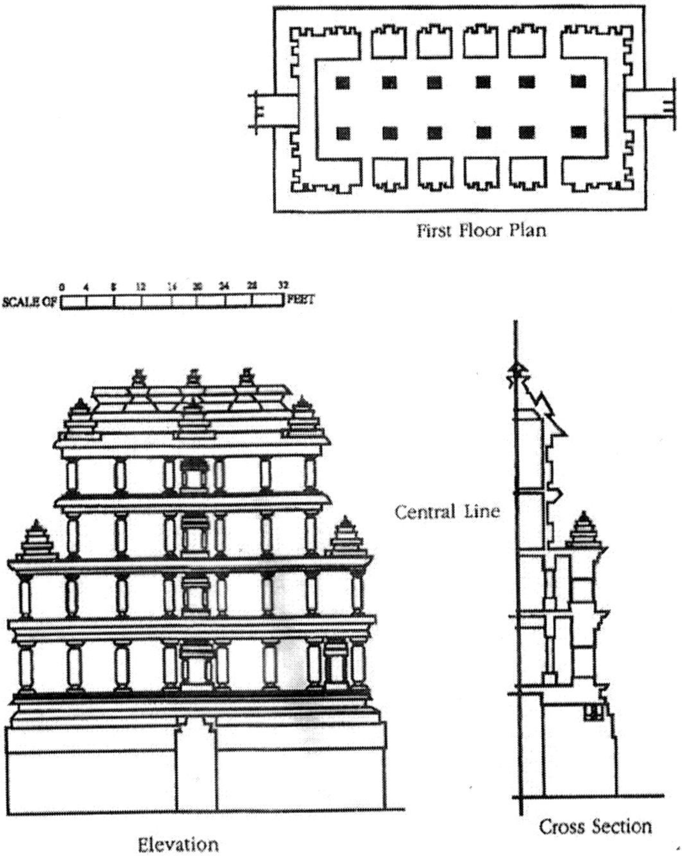

Dvara-Harmy (Gate-Edifice) Fourth Court for Temples & Residential Earthquake Resistance

Diagram 14

Five-Storey buildings had also been divided in equal proportion as shown in Diagram No. 15. In all the structures we observe that the plinth height is equal to ground floor to make the structure safer and long lasting.

For Five-Storeys

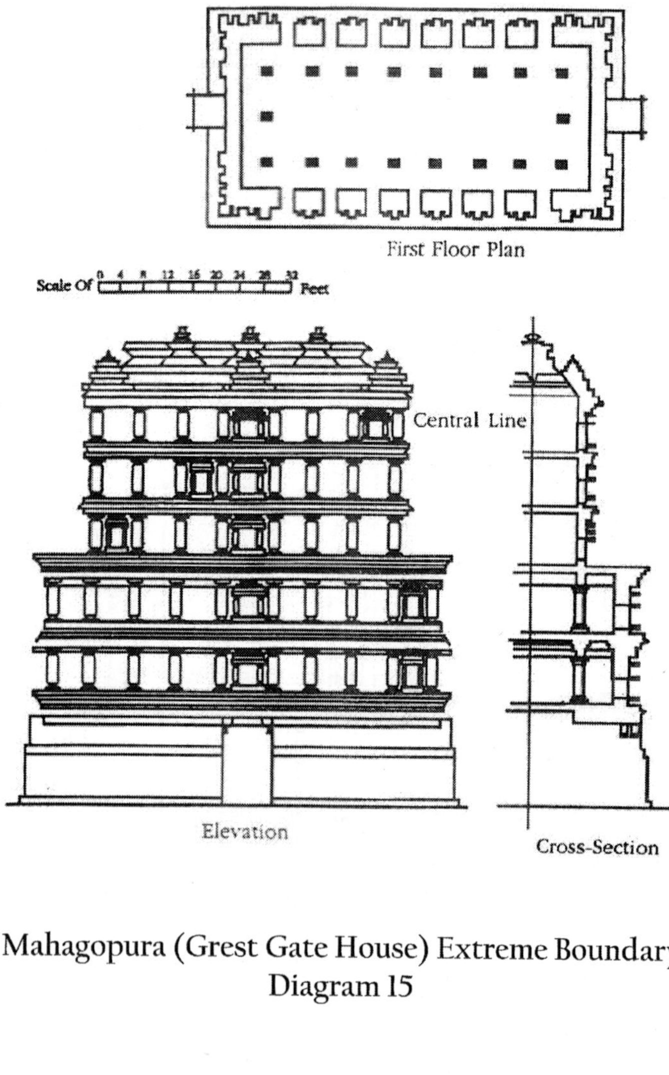

Mahagopura (Grest Gate House) Extreme Boundary
Diagram 15

Timber Work of Temple

A very special and seasoned wood was after used for timber work of temples. All joints were wooden. Their tradition was not to use nail or screw for the jointary job. As per the principle of Vastu it was said that the positive energy comes from the main entry gate, door frame (chokhat) must be good seasoned wood with four members frame that too much without using any nail or screw. Refer Diagram No. 16 and 17.

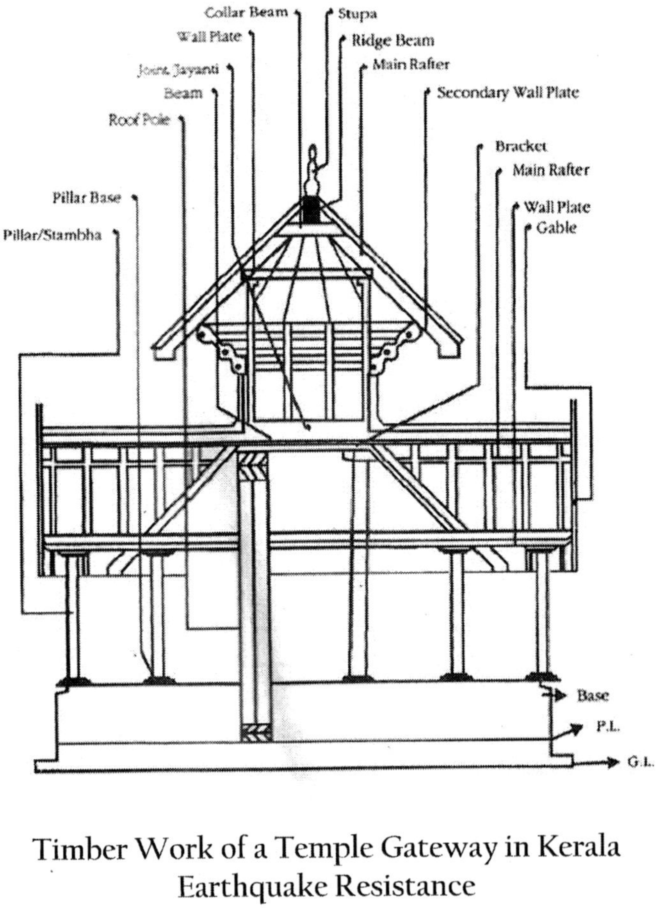

Timber Work of a Temple Gateway in Kerala
Earthquake Resistance
(Ref: Mayamatam – Vol. 1, p. 16, Fig. 14)
Diagram 16

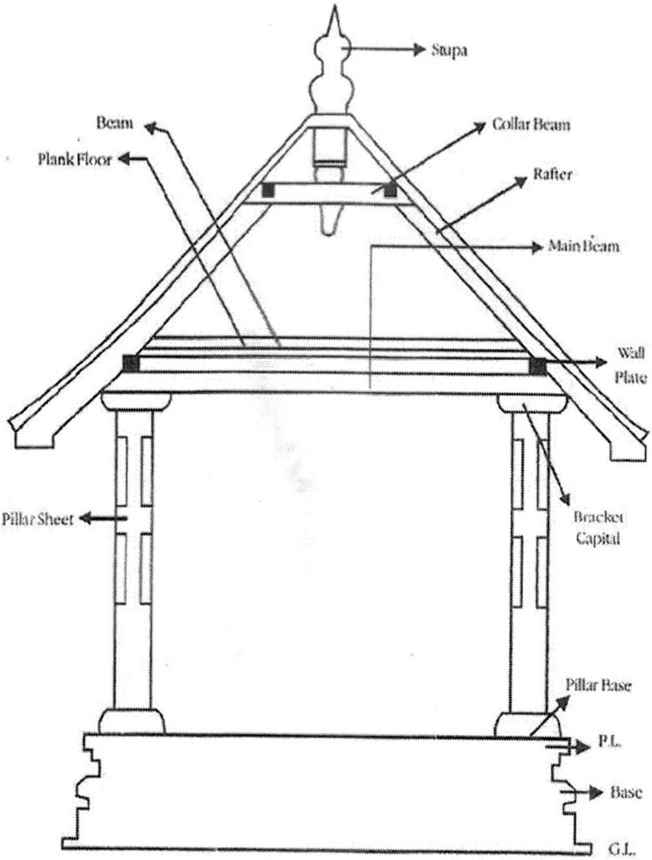

Timber Work of a Pavilion with a Pyramidal Roof in Kerala Earthquake Resistance
(Ref: Mayamatam: Vol. 1, p. Lxv, Fig. 13)
Diagram 17

Learning from the past and requirement of present, we can combine the present and past and create a new design for 21th century for a peaceful prayer hall Refer Diagram No. 18, 19 and 20.

Front Elevation

Proposed Prayer hall for 21st Century

Diagram 18

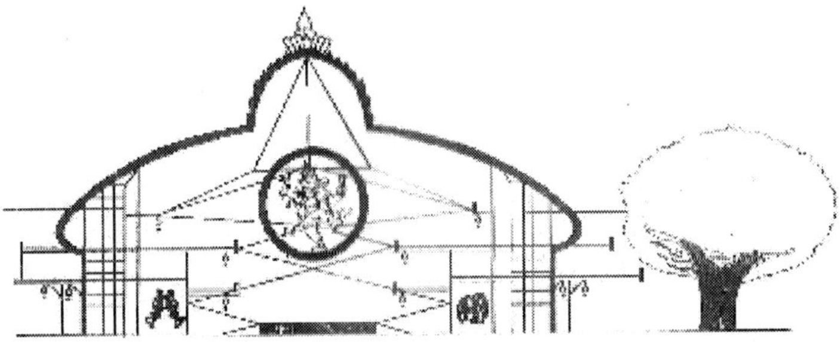

Diagram 19

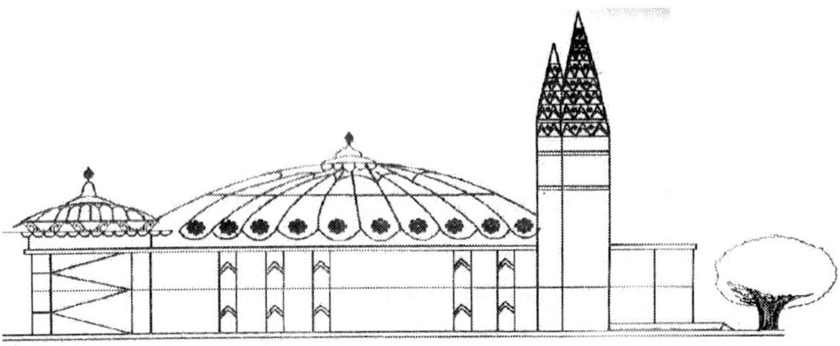

Side View-Section

Temple

COMPLEX

Diagram 20

Orientation (Face) of Building Gate/ Main Gate or Entry Door

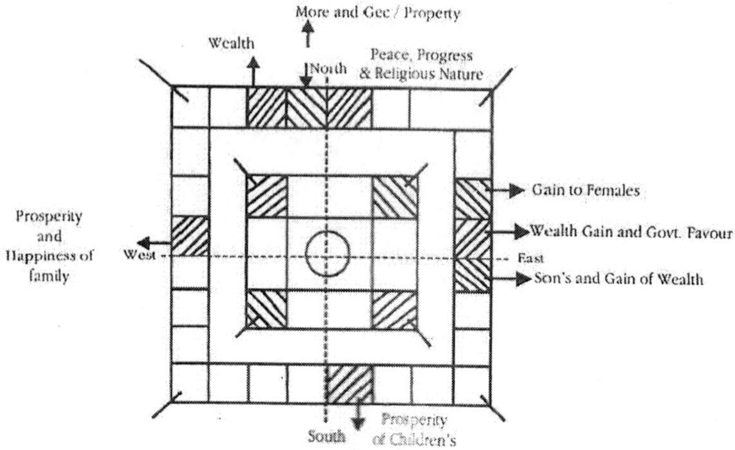

On the Basis of Birth Sign-Rashi of Head owner of the House.

North	South	West	East
Aries	Gemini	Taurus	Cancer
Leo	Virgo	Libra	Scorpio
Sagittarius	Capricorn	Aquarius	Pisces

Note: Just in front of the Gate/Door there should not be any of the following obstructions:

- Temple, Gurudwara, Mosque, Church etc.
- Corner of neighbor building, septic tank, main Sewerage.
- A lane or road, tree, electric pole, pillar, ladders are considered inauspicious.

If/or keep more than twice distance from the building height.

The position of main entry gate as per Vastu Zodiac Sign.

12

Vastu Shastra the Vedic Philosophy V/S Modern Architecture

The term 'Vastu' is defined as Vasnati Praninah Yatra or a place where living beings reside. It is presided over by the Vastospati, the steady one, king of gods, Indra. So, before a house is built, oblations are offered to Indra (wielder of the thunderbolt), Varuna (Lord of rains), and Vayu (Lord of winds). Man builds to seek shelter from these powerful forces. Since Yama (Lord of death) also rule the world, he, too, is to be invoked when man builds his small world. In the Vedas, there is a special veneration of the central post, for it is considered a symbol of the Vastospati. Perhaps, this is an extension of the ancient habitat under a tree which, in the most primitive house, led to the structure being built over and around a central post. The raising of the vamsa (beam) over the sthuna (post) is a sacred act during which hymns from the Atharvaveda are recited. The tenets of the Vedas, thus, considered the building of a house, a religious act. A man's private expression-his house – if built a4ccording to traditional principles, would enrich his public life by bringing him prosperity and contentment.

The Vastushastras are a record of these oral traditional that was, in the ancient times, best known to the Sthapati (architects). The Shastras incorporated the course of the sun, the moon and the planet, thus symbolizing recurrent time cycles within a house. The house was located correctly in space and time as it incorporated the mathematical and physical science of astrology. Texts like the Arthashastras also included the concept of bye-laws by describing the position of drains, boundary walls, and well/tube well opening and gateways. Spaces between houses, the location of opening in a house, façade treatment and even sanitary regulations were specified. The violation of these laws was punishable by the state which was more than what can be said about modern building bye-laws.

Some broad principles can identify that even today guide the design of the house. These apply to site selection, site planning, the house plan, openings, structure and proportions.

Site Selection

The best shape is square, rectangular, or circular. A triangular site or one with an odd number of sides is to be strictly avoided, though this can be amended by adding a small additional side. Pundits today recommend a four-sided site, tapering to the north-east. A site is considered propitious that drains water from the south-west to the north-east. However, since most urban housing sites are rectangular and sulas (obstructions) can be amended, site selection today does not usually involve a Pundit. Various other tests mentioned in the Grihyasutra primarily for determining soil quality are rarely, if ever, performed today, as building materials come from areas far away from site, and poor soil quality can be easily compensated.

The Site Plan

The site or the Vastu is regarded as the body of a demi-god, the Vastupurusha or Vastunara, subjugated by the gods. Each victorious god holds down a part of this demon so that he would never rise again. The gods, as well as the Vastupurusha himself, have to be propitiated while building a house. It is said that the Vastupurusha requested Brahma to always occupy the centre of his being, the nabhi or the navel. Interestingly, Brahma also represents the third dimension above ground level, while Vasuki is the god of the depths. The Vastupursha's head faces north-east while his feet are towards south-east. Consequently, the north-east portion of the site has assumed a sacred status and is given a great deal of importance during planning. The Vastu is inhabited by the eight main gods of the eight cardinal directions, while the Padas or divisions between these cardinals are occupied by the lesser gods. The gods of the cardinals have a major influence on the design process, but the lesser gods are not considered unless a person goes in for elaborate sculptural decoration of his house.

The Vastupurusha Mandala is a square yantra, a diagram, representing the ritual form of the Vastupurusha. It seeks to represent the macrocosm, the essence of all things, the Supreme Being, the Purusha, in the microcosm, man, the Purusha. The Mandala can be of various divisions or Pada. There were 64 Pada Mandalas for villages, palaces of kings and towns, 49 Pada Mandalas for wells, tanks, and ponds and 1,000 Pada Mandalas for forts and cities.

According to the Shastras, while constructing a house a minimum amount of space should be left on the south and the west sides of the site and maximum space on the north and east sides. However, the introduction of by-laws on a site with restricted amount of space can cause problems in a south or west facing site. For instance, in order to follow a bye-law that specifies a 10-foot frontage, this principle has to be broken, losing in the process the coveted backyard, though gaining a front yard. Fortunately, people are not such sticklers for privacy today as they were in the olden days.

The Grihyasutra also mentions the position and types of trees to be planted on the site. The basic rule followed today is that of planting the tallest trees on the south-west section of the site and shorter shrubbery on the other sides. Since in a hot climate like ours, the sun is on the south at midday, tall trees which provide ample shade are grown on the south-west part of the site. When the sun sets, its angle is low and the shrubbery serves as a useful shading device on the north and west sides.

The House Plan

While a square house is considered auspicious, most geometrical shapes are allowed. One of the stipulations is that the corners should not be cut as this is inauspicious and attracts evil spirits. In any case, corners are structurally awkward and should not be tempered with. The exceptions are the north-east corner which can be additions can be made. For example, in House the south-west corner is actually cut out, but an extended verandah rectifies the problem.

The divinities associated with the cardinal points play a significant role in the planning of the house. Since the north-east represents the gate of heaven, the puja room and the kitchen must be located in that part of the site. The kitchen should be placed on the south-east or north-west, but the stove gas, agni must face east. The west represents the darkness, Varuna, and the south, Yama, Lord of death.

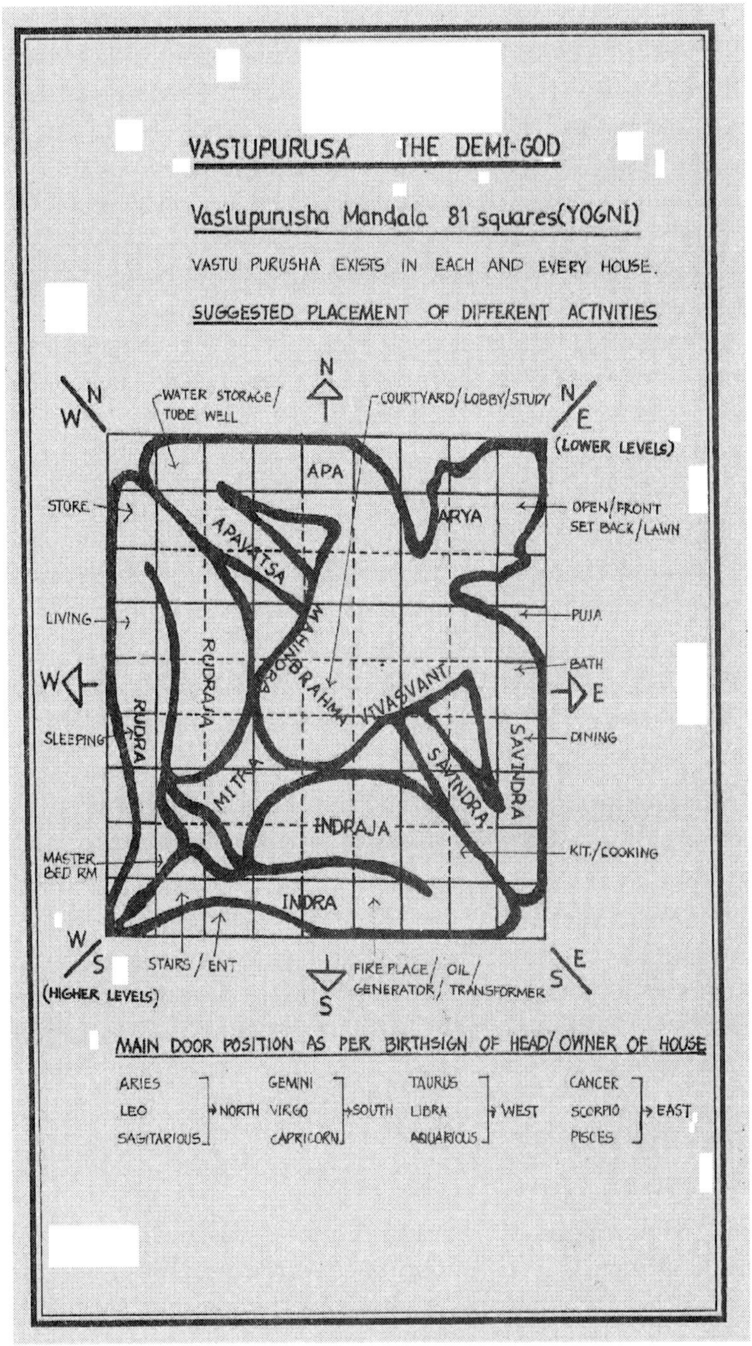
VASTUPURUSA THE DEMI-GOD
Vastupurusha Mandala 81 squares(YOGNI)
VASTU PURUSHA EXISTS IN EACH AND EVERY HOUSE.
SUGGESTED PLACEMENT OF DIFFERENT ACTIVITIES
N
W N
N E
(LOWER LEVELS)
WATER STORAGE/ TUBE WELL
COURTYARD/LOBBY/STUDY
APA
ARYA
APAVATSA
STORE
OPEN/FRONT SET BACK/LAWN
LIVING
PUJA
MAHINDRA
BRAHMA
RUDRAJA
VIVASVANT
W
BATH
E
RUDRA
SAVINDRA
SAVITRA
SLEEPING
DINING
MITRA
INDRAJA
KIT./COOKING
MASTER BED RM
INDRA
W S
(HIGHER LEVELS)
STAIRS / ENT
FIRE PLACE / OIL / GENERATOR / TRANSFORMER
S
S E
MAIN DOOR POSITION AS PER BIRTHSIGN OF HEAD/OWNER OF HOUSE
ARIES LEO SAGITARIOUS → NORTH
GEMINI VIRGO CAPRICORN → SOUTH
TAURUS LIBRA AQUARIOUS → WEST
CANCER SCORPIO PISCES → EAST

The south-west is dedicated to the Pitra (ancestors) representing exit from life. This corner is considered the ideal location for the master bedroom–at the feet of the Vastupurusha. The sacred north-east corner should not be desecrated by toilets or the master bedroom (the location of the conjugal bed). The centre of the house, its Garbhagriha, the womb of the higher self, has a special significance, especially in a geometrically centralized space. This could be symbolized by using a courtyard or a tulsi manch and is open to architectural interpretation. In House X, a skylight symbolizes this womb. However, the rules are not binding and the ultimate choice of location left to the builder of the house.

The basic grid locates the sleeping spaces on the south and west, the living spaces on the south and the cooking and dining spaces on the north and east. The staircase must face east or west, never north or south – possibly a mythical association where north- south was associated with night and death. However, certain modifications have been negotiated these days by making the first step face east or west, so that a person at least starts climbing while facing east or west.

Openings

The total number of doors and windows must be even. Doors are assigned a special symbolic value in the Grihyasutra. A door on the east brings fame and strength, on the north, children and cattle, and on the south, wealth and fame. A door on the west is to be best avoided as it brings misfortune (evidently, any spillover of activity on the western side of the house. It should also be the first in a sequence of doors leading to the back door – all on the centre line. Considering that the breeze usually comes in from the south, this is a good way of ensuring cross- ventilation.

Structure

The trabeated of post and beam was deemed worthy of veneration in the Vedas. The posts were especially important as they were compared to gods in the support that they afforded. A thousands-pillared hall, therefore, was considered sacred. Each post in conjunction with its cardinal point took on a symbolic value. The eastern post represented truth and faith, the southern post, sacrifices and gifts, the western post, strength and power, and the northern post, represented truth and faith, the southern post, sacrifice and gifts, Brahmins and Kshtriyas. This symbolism was extended to other parts of the structure as well. The pinnacle represented fortune, the chief post law, the door jambs day and night, while the foundation represented the bull and the ocean. Though such symbolism seems abstruse, it indicates the importance that the structure of the house had for its builder. For, every one of these parts had to be strong if the house was to be stable and long lasting.

Proportions

The texts evolved elaborate proportioning systems, whereby the sizes of the building blocks were also standardized. The system of measurement was anthropometric based on the angula (finger), hasta (hand), etc. such a system simplified the process of construction considered by making available a reliable method of proportioning the pillars, facades and roofs. Classification of house types was also possible, and included Prasads (with high roofs of Shikharas, or pinnacles), Soudhas (polished buildings) and Karnaltas (houses with domes). Today, no such system is followed. Perhaps, this is way our urban environment leaves much to be desired by way of aesthetics. The only rule that modern Pundits insist on is that the south-western corner must have the maximum height and the north-eastern corner the minimum height. This is an extension of the basic rule of the site having its highest point at the south-west and lowest point at the north-east.

In its widest sense, Vastu was anything made with skill. Not only houses, buildings, temples and towns, but also roads, drains, ponds, well, furniture and colorful ornaments painting. It offered a multi-disciplinary approach to the process of design. This, perhaps, is what we must learn from the Vastu Shastra – to provide a framework for design that maintains standards.

13

The Cosmic Vision of Colors

A human can see from his naked eye the materialistic world and the colorful nature. But he cannot see within himself the soul inside him. To understand and to be a part of the nature and to attain spiritual awakening, man, therefore, must awaken himself, specifically for the persons who are professionally involved for creative jobs – fields like Architect, Artist, Scientist, Designer, Sculptor, Builders, etc.

Chakras–*What they signify and how to read them?*

A Chakra is particular point at the human body where the life energy, or spiritual body, or the soul, comes into closer contact with the physical body.

There are many such Chakras in the body, but major seven color Chakras are located in the ascending order, as shown in the illustration. (Dig. 1)

1. At the Crown
2. At the brow (between the two eyebrows)
3. At the throat (near the thyroid)
4. Near the heart
5. At the solar plexus
6. At the navel
7. At the gonads (coccyx, the last bone of the vertebral column)

Each of these Chakras has a color associated with it by virtue of its vibrations through the brain-wave. There are other types of radiations on even shorter wavelengths which cannot be seen by the human eye, for example Radio or TV Waves, X-ray, Remote and other such colors and sound waves, ultraviolet rays, etc. which are present in their natural form in the atmosphere.

Below is discussed one by one these seven Chakras starting from coccyx:

1. The root Chakra at the gonads is associated with red color, corresponds to one's energy and motivation. If suffers imbalance when a person becomes impatient, angry, violent, over-manipulative, revengeful or sexually obsessed over the better of one's thoughts and actions.
2. The navel Chakra corresponds to courage and confidence and vibrates to the color of orange. With the negative emotions which can block this centre are feelings of materialism, pomposity, cruelty and sluggishness.
3. The solar plexus Chakra, corresponding to one's career and profession, vibrates to yellow and is seriously affected by laziness, cowardice, cynicism and criticism.
4. This Chakra near the heart must be kept free of jealousy, possessiveness, insecurity, envy, vibrates to pink and green color, and is the centre of one's relationships.
5. The throat Chakra at the thyroid gland level often gets blocked by depression, feelings of isolation, inability to communicate and accept changes. It is the centre of one's communication, unhampered by negativity – vibrates to blue color.
6. The Chakra at brow is blocked in most of the modern people by their day-to-day actions, attitudes and thoughts of fear, retaining grudges and maintaining an unforgiving attitude towards others leaning towards the materialistic

world and away from natural life. In the Vedic period, it was the other way. People had a leaning towards spiritual world and lived a very simple and natural life. This Chakra vibrates to indigo and is the seat of institution, as explained in the early chapter.

7. The crown Chakra vibrates to violet and is the seat of enlightenment, if one succeeds in pushing away arrogance, conceit and hunger for power and control.

If we keep on regular practice to keep our chakras UNBLOCKED, a deep understanding of humanity and peace in the entire universe is ours. Incongruous by one's own actions, as the colors are only the result of one's mental and physical activities, a human makes its own beautiful AURA. The idea aura, of course, should be white as described in the Vedas and that depicted by the saints and pious persons.

What is Aura

Aura consists of different colors. The aura is defined as a luminous radiation, light around a person's head or body. Most people are unable to see aura as clearly as they see their surroundings, because aura consists of different colors.

The aura may be likened to a barometer of the physical and spiritual bodies because it reveals not just the physical condition of the body, but also the state of spiritual development.

It is relevant to explain here that the human eye perceives the spectrum of light from a wavelength of about 400 nanometers (one nanometer equal to billionth of a meter) of deep red color, up to approximate 700 nanometer of deep violet. Between these parameters was a wavelength along which the rainbow spectrum of colors is visible.

The different colors appearing in the aura have been studied by physics, and various tints of each color suggest different characteristics.

For an experiment study, the author designed the First DISCOTHEQUE in India in 1968.

The characteristics of different colors in relation to human habits

RED: Dark red means a violent temper and inner turmoil in the color nervous system. A domineering person usually has a generous amount of dark red in his aura. Light red suggests an active person who is nervous as well as egocentric. An overblown ego is apparent in scarlet, and immaturity shows itself through pink color. Pink always appears in the auras of children, and in an adult, apart from immaturity, it suggests a childish preoccupation with oneself.

ORANGE: Its golden shade suggests self-control, but the brownish tint of orange clearly shows an indifferent attitude to everything, suggesting laziness. Too much orange may indicate kidney ailments.

YELLOW: Golden yellow indicates good health, a person who is not prone to anxieties, who is friendly. A sort of ruby yellow denotes an inferiority complex.

GREEN: Successful and dedicated healers usually have emerald green in their auras. A slightly bluish green indicates helpfulness and trustworthiness, but a lemony green is a certain sign of deceit.

BLUE: Deeper shades of blue denote persons who are happy in their chosen field of work. Pale blue shows a lack of depth in the person, and the aquamarine type of auric blue indicates the diligent worked.

INDIGO AND VIOLET: Both colors represent "seekers" of truth. Once they have found what they are seeking, be it religious convictions or career slots of their choice, these colors glide back to a deep blue. If there is auric purple, it reveals an overbearing person, and also suggests the possibilities of cardiac and stomach ailments.

If we go back to the Vedic period, you might be surprised to discover that, on some particular day or on different festivals, they wear particular color of clothes or particular color of flower or add particular color to their food. Similarly, on different sacred or religious ceremonies, they use particularly different colors of flower, clothes and color wash on their house and walls.

Even in the 20th century, you can see different color Chakras every morning that Hindus make in front of their homes, particularly in South India.

More details in depth of colors are explained on next chapter 'How Colors Influence the Human Mind and Body'. Also I explain the importance of colors in Human life and his living style by choosing the color scheme of his House, Living Room, Bed Room, Kitchen, Bathroom and also his working place.

Vastu play a very important role by choosing the colors of different direction of walls etc.

14

Cosmic Energy from Air, Light and Color

Exposure to Sunlight

Sunlight and fresh air is the basic element form which all life originates, develops, heals and evolves. The body is a living cell which is stimulated and regulated by light. It has a profound effect on the regulation of human physiological and emotional functioning and the development of our consciousness. Light effectively enhances learning abilities, strengthens the immunizing properties and plays a role in the extension of life. Energies developed by Sun, Light and Air play a vital role in formation of principles of Vastu Shastra.

Sunlight is composed of variety of energies that are transmitted to Earth in the form of electromagnetic waves. Only a small portion of these waves actually reach the Earth's surface and only about one percent of the total electromagnetic spectrum is perceived by the eyes. This visible portion of the electromagnetic spectrum, containing all the colors of the rainbow from violet (with the largest wavelength) to red (with the shortest wavelength) is a most important key to human functioning and evolution. Our lives, health and well being are truly dependent on the sun.

Sunlight is a holistic approach for the development of physiological, emotional and spiritual bodies. The profound human evolution in some deep way is related to our ability to take in and utilize light on physical and spiritual level. The vision of our sages of the past is not different from the scientific discoveries of the present. Sunlight, our source of light, warmth and energy, not only sustains all life on Earth, but it sustains the Earth itself. It provides plans with the energy of photosynthesis, which in turn sustains life on Earth.

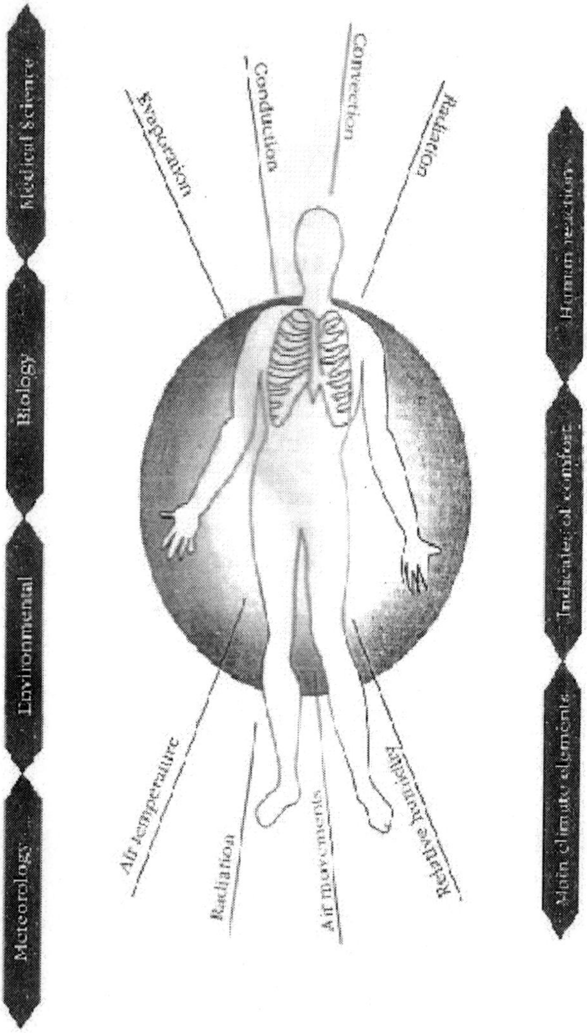

Diagram 1

Exposure to Sunlight

- Producing Vitamin D in the body.
- Normal growth and development of bones.
- Decrease Blood Sugar.
- Balance Blood Pressure.
- Decrease resting heart rate.
- Decrease respiratory rate.
- Decrease Lactic Acid in blood.
- Increase resistance to Arthritis.

Yoga and Meditation

- Increase energy and strength in the body.
- Increase tolerance to stress.
- Balance the breathing rhythm.
- Increase ability of blood to absorb and carry oxygen.
- Increase storage of oxygen.

Rhythm of Life with Changing Color

From sunrise to sunset environmental color changes and correspondingly effect all living things. The very first sunrise to the sunset of the present, we continued to be awed by the beauty, power, life-creating and life sustaining properties emanating from light. It would appear, and then that our physiological and emotional centers are synchronized with nature by way of light and that we truly seem to be the offspring of nature. Based on the awareness that daily color variations in the environment are intimately connected to the body's daily rhythmic changes, humans have recognized that the season color changes also reflect biological alterations with in all living things. Harmony within our life processes is related to the level of communication between out body and the environment. Unbalanced responses to specific rhythms, seasons and their associated cycles are related to specific kinds of physical and emotional problems. Longevity may be related to our ability to our ability to integrate and synchronize ourselves with the planetary and solar-stellar energies that surround us. In humans, exposure to sunlight significantly influences physiological and psychological functions. Among these, fertility and mood are two most profoundly affected. Light has played a consistent role in the development of all living things. More recently, Albert Szent Gyorgyi, Nobel prize winner and the discover of Vitamin C, has recognized how profoundly color and light affect us. From his work he concluded that "all the energy which we take into our bodies is derived from the sun." he saw that, through the process of photosynthesis, the sun's energy is stored in plans which are in turn eaten by eaten by animals and oxygen released is taken in by humans. Sun is a source of mental energy and the best minds evolved in a natural process where the sun was temperate. Not very hot, not very cold, just the right temperature (+ or -3) of 24o c. the hot sun has glare, sharp light and dark shadows. Cool sun has colors and cold sun rarely rises above horizon or often geographically couples with heavy clouds in the sky snow on earth generally, gloomy but beautiful, silvery and long hours of twilight. Hot humid zones with heavy cloudy sky for a longer period of the year also have distinctive culture and architecture. Sun has played an important role in development of visual qualities of architecture in terms of textures, color, roof forms and above in all expressions of vitality.

Scientific Discovery

The human body is nourished directly by the stimulation of the sunlight or nourished directly by eating foods, drinking fluids or breathing air that has been vitalized by the sun's light energy. Dr. Zame Kime, in his book "Sunlight", states that a series of exposure to sunlight will decrease resting heart rate, blood pressure, respiratory rate, blood sugar and lactic acid in the blood following exercise; and help increase in energy, strength, endurance, tolerance to stress and ability of the blood to absorb and carry oxygen. The human body is truly a living photocell that is energized by the sun's light, the nutrient of humankind. Szent Gyorgyi discovered that May enzymes and hormones involved in processing this energy are color responsive and very sensitive to light. He added that light striking the body can literally alter the basic biological functions involved in processing the body's fuel, which powers our lives. Martinek and Brezin in 1979 found that (a) colors of light can stimulate certain bodily enzymes to be 500 percent more effective and (b) some colors can increase the rate of enzymatic reactions, activate or deactivate certain enzyme. Light not only affects us but our state of consciousness determines how we use light.

Use Sunlight for Our Health

Sunlight has been used by all the major historical culture and it has touched the hearts and creative minds of those who have learned to appreciate its potential. It wasn't until the 1800s that physicians throughout the world became fully aware of the healing properties of sunlight. At this point in time, cures using light were being claimed for conditions ranging from simple inflammation and paralysis to tuberculosis. It was later discovered that sunlight striking the skin initiated a series of reactions in the body leading to the production of Vitamin D, a necessary ingredient for the absorption of calcium and other minerals from the diet. If Vitamin D is absent, the body will not absorb the amount of calcium required for normal growth and development of bones. In 1903 Neils Finsen of Denmark was awarded the

Noble Prize for being the first person to successfully treat skin tuberculosis with ultraviolet light. During his many years of work with both sunlight and ultraviolet light, Finsen reported miraculous cures on thousands of patients.

The cosmic cycles affect our universe, which then affects the Solar system, which then affects the Earth and so on down through Earth's climate, seasons, inhabitants, right down to the smallest particle within an atom.

Since all things are integrally connected in this way, everything affects each other. Nothing escapes this process. Universally occurring variation affects all living things. Nature has a master plan for us to spend part of our lives exploring our external environments and part of our lives exploring our internal environments.

What Veda Says?

Since most of the modern population spends its working hours indoors eliminating the morning sunlight and fresh air from their daily intake, it is very important to discuss and discover the indoor environment particularly in 21st Century, where the environment throughout the world is becoming more and more polluted, in relation to our health, productivity and in general universal peace and well-being. If the absence or imbalance of certain naturally present spectral light components causes a reduction in our physiological, emotional and intellectual functioning, light must play an integral role in the proper biological functioning of all living organism.

In this regard Vastu plays a very important role in helping clean environment for the building, free from pollution of any king, full of light and color needed by balancing the Five Elements of Nature.

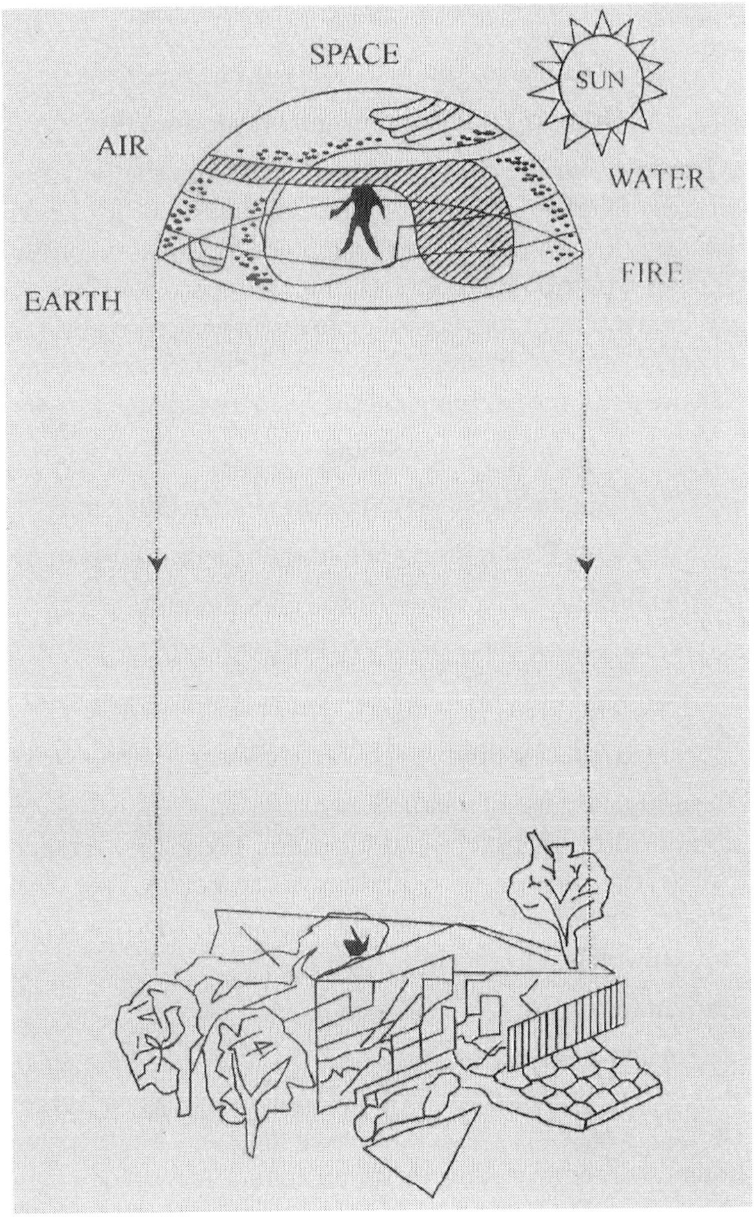

Theoretical Approach to Balance Shelter in Line with Five Elements

Diagram 2

Sloka

Na Pranena Na Apranena MatyoJivati Kaschana I

Itarena Tu Jivanti Yasmin Etavapritau II

Meaning: Our life doesn't depend merely on the breathing process. The intake of diet is in deed important for health, but health does not rest on food alone, because everything can be thrown out of order if the mind is upset. A turbulence injected into the mind is enough to disturb the entire balance of personality. Your strength is in you. Religion begins where science ends; the beginning of the higher wisdom.

Sloka

Sbastrenanena Sarvasya Lokasya Param Sukham I

Chaturvarga Phalaprapti ssallokashch Bhaveddhruvam II

Shilp Shastra Parigyanmartyoapi Suratam Vrajet I

Paramanad Janakasya Devanamidmiritam II

Shilpam Vina Na hi Jagattrishu Lokeshu Vidyate I

Jagad Vina Na Shilpam ch Vertate Vasav !prabho! II

Meaning: Because of Vastu Shastra, the whole Universe gets good health, happiness and all-round prosperity.. Human beings attain divinity with this knowledge. Followers of Vastu Shastra get not only worldly pleasures but also experience heavenly bliss.

Radiant Energy

Ancient civilizations apparently knew about light, namely its route of entry into the body and some of its major effects on the body's regulatory centers and their functions. Major control enters of the body are directly stimulated and regulated by light, to an extent far beyond what modern science, until recently, has been willing to accept. Though the body's balance is regulated by autonomic nervous system which is regulated by an important part of the brain, the hypothalamus, which receives light energy through eyes, co-ordinates and regulates most of our life sustaining functions and also initiates and direct our reactions and adaption to stress.

Many of us spend our lifetime chasing mental images rather than observing the realities of life. The general lack of awareness has already led to the toxification of life's most important basic elements: light, air, food and water. Light is the major nutrient sustaining all life and it follows that poor and/or incomplete lighting will significantly affect every aspect of human existence. It is important to initially look at the constituents of sunlight as well as the kinds of artificial light to which we are exposed in our daily lives.

Monolithic Status of Gomateshwar in Situ Granite and Five Senses

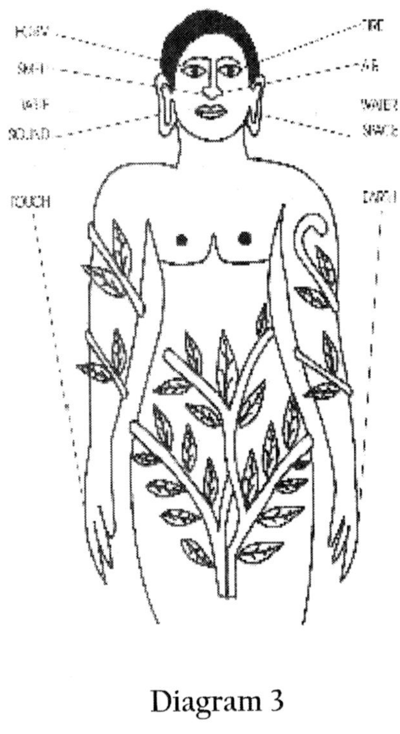

Diagram 3

Light is composed of waves of radiant energy. Sunlight, which contains all the different wavelengths, provides the total electromagnetic spectrum under which all life on this planet has evolved. Until 1879, when Edison perfected the light bulb, people spent most of their time outdoors and received adequate daily doses of natural full spectrum sunlight. The light bulb became largely an "indoor event", which drastically reduced the amount of time to which people exposed themselves to full spectrum sunlight.

Since most of us spend our working hours indoors, eliminating sunlight from our daily diets, it is important to find this indoor environment in relation to our health, and productivity in general.

Seven Stage of Human Awareness

Chanchalam hi manah Krishna pramahti balavaddridham II

Means: Oh! Lord the man is chanchal. It cannot stay firm. 'Mann' (thought) travels at the speed much more than sound or light and takes you thousands of miles away. This can be controlled by meditation. Our heart (Mann) always misguides you. The above five senses do their duties regularly without knowing what are good or bad. The eye will see any type of scene, ears will listen any type of sound without knowing whether it is good or bad smell, similarly touch and taste do their job.

Our brain (buddhi) controls all the senses and tells whether our experience is good or bad. For the above education (gyan) one has to train the brain to judge between good and bad. Above all is Atma (soul). All the above five stages are within your control, you can train them, control them the way you want by doing regular practice. Whatever training you give, you get the consequential result.

But above this is Atma (the soul), which is beyond your control. It is independent; it does not die with you. So, if you make friendship with the soul by understanding it, you become a Rishi. Away from this materialistic world, you become very close to him. And above all, comes the seventh stage where Atma is lean (blended) with Maha Atma i.e.(Param Atma, Paramatma) in this stage I and You become He, there is no difference between I and You, all are one and this triangle becomes circle. We are the bindu, a point of start. When I and You become one, we become love, we are not in love, but we are love. You always say you are my life, I give my heart to you, and you are without ego. So, I, You and He become one, neither you are attached or detached with this materialistic world and enjoy all stages of awareness.

To be in discipline always sound difficult. Everyone says that to be in discipline is very difficult but I always say that it is very easy to be in discipline. What is Discipline? Formation of Human Habits?

1. Good Habit which is as per environment and liked by everyone is being in discipline.
2. Bad Habits are not liked by others and according to the environment means that you are not in Discipline.

Everyone has certain habits and if you develop with practice and add some more good habits. Everybody says you are a much disciplined person and you will be successful in all fields and like by everyone.

15

How Colors Influence the Human Mind and Body

Definition of Color

Colors are the name given to distinguish the various sensations which light at various rates of vibration effects on the eye. Color is also used to denote the property of bodies that causes them to emit the light that affects our senses.

The use of color, however, extends even further back, perhaps as much as 1, 50,000 to 2, 00,000 years. In the Vedic period, all colors were taken out from vegetables and flowers, which were more permanent in shade, soothing to the eye and had a natural tint. Even now in many parts of the world, instead of using synthetic color, vegetable colors are used, particularly in textile printing and making design, miniature painting, ceramic, etc.

Ice age man buried his dead in red or painted their bones with red colors, that the flow of red blood meant the difference between life and death. Probably, they believed that the color red itself was, therefore, life giving. The Egyptians used colors obtained from metals found in the earth, plants, insects and fishes.

Names of the colors were derived from that of plants, geographic names, and natural phenomena, man-made products and miscellaneous objects. Like in plants apricot yellow, grass green and rose red while Berlin blue, Spanish green and Naples yellow are geographic names. Name of colors under man-made products are chocolate brown, wine red and bottle green. Under green and miscellaneous objects offer us calypso red, ultra-violet and also infra-red.

Colors as Symbol

At a very early period in the human history, the symbolic use of colors was made. Heart was colored red during the early period which was the seat of life and the blood was identified with life and consciousness. Yellow was possibly the color of fire, white that of day and black that of night and death, from past till today, there has been continuation in the symbolic use of colors, as we associate red with parades and games, blue with that of outstanding work, purple as of and dignity and reverence, green with nature and healing, yellow of sunshine and of course pink to good health.

Colors and the Human Glands

- A particular color can actives or can control human glands by different bodily functions. Such as for a good appetizer for the good habit, or to give excitement for the low blood pressure patient, a red family color atmosphere is recommended. Similarly, blue color is to top overeating habit.
- For a high blood pressure patient, a light limited soothing color atmosphere is recommended. In a hospital, white color is used for hygienic reasons, but for healing, doctors use green color in operation theatre. For a good healthy/ tasty food, a golden yellow, white and green color is recommended.
- The colors are divided into two main group – that of primary and secondary colors. The primary colors are greenish-blue or turquoise, yellow and magenta red. The secondary colors are the primaries in paints. Colors are further sub-divided into five categories as that of hue, shade, tint, tone and complementary colors.

- A color that is brilliant and has no black or white hue, like that of yellow, red blue and green. A color that is made with mixing a hue and white is known as tint, such as pink and ivory colors. A color that is mixture of pure hue, black and white is called tone.
- The two colors that can make white are complementary colors. While grey are tones and greenish-blue or turquoise and orange-red are complementary colors, also yellow, violet-blue, magenta red and green.

Effect of Color on our Mind and Body

Colors affect our body and mind very much, as explained earlier. The purest and most thoughtful minds are those which live colors the most. The cool colors are blue sea or mainly blue in cast. The warm colors are red or mainly red and yellow in cast. Red makes you feel gay, while man can work best when surrounding by blue, but too strong a blue or red can even become depressing. People often feel cold in a blue room and warm in a red room. It is the color that makes them feel that way.

Red is the most popular color. Next to red is blue, then green, and yellow follows. Red and magenta red is the most popular color with girl and women. Among boys and men, orange-red is more liked. In blue, a woman likes turquoise best and men prefer deep blue. Dark colors absorb light and heat, whereas bright colors reflect light and heat.

Research has named as many as millions of color variation between neutral white, grey and black. A color attains its true appearance in a good daylight. As an observer looks at several colors at the same time, stimulus to his eyes changes and pleasant or unpleasant sensations may result. Yellow light by nature includes most of the spectrum, while violet and red which only include one extreme end of a spectrum seems dark or very light by nature.

16

Living with Colors (for Happy & Healthy Living)

Pleasing decoration in home can be made by using a variety of colors, all of which are mixed with entirely complex, hues. Greenish blue mixed with white or with grey makes a beautiful wall color and against this background colors with orange in it will look the best, because of its being a complementary color with which brown furniture will look excellent.

Decorating an interior man's tuning of colors. A bed room is intended for rest and the colors therefore should be delicate tints or tones- soft, calm and restful. A living room, however, can be more dramatic with more concentrating colored objects. The baby's room should have pure bright colors because babies can see only bright colors.

That is way a room with poor daylight should be painted in light color. If the room gets a good amount of natural light throughout the day, it can be painted in some deep color. If a room has only a north window, which admits cold light, we should not use blue on the walls. If a room gets too much direct sunlight, it is not advisable to paint the walls yellow or peach. It is nearly always better to have the ceiling white because a white ceiling reflects much heat and light into a room.

Some colored lamps and shades produce curious effects. A person's face appears ghastly when seen by light passing through a blue shade, since there is an absence of red and warm tints which produce the normal healthy appearance of the face. The red carpet will reflect more red rays by artificial light and will appear to be of a stronger red at night than that of day, but a blue carpet is a more intense blue in day time than in the night. Purple colors contain red and blue both.

Color contrast in value is perhaps the most important factor in a composition or a design maximum contrast is obtained by the use of colors of extremely strong chromes. A strong yellow on a black field is an excellent example of maximum visibility. A bright strong yellowish red would be considered as a powerful color. The color of an object depends upon the light it emits or sends back to the eyes. Opposite contrast colors are quickly changed when mixed, as for black which makes colors both brighter and lighter in looks.

Surrounding an intense color with a grey increases the apparent colorfulness of the intense color making. It appears even brighter or brilliant. Surrounded by yellow, a grey color may appear slightly blue. Surrounding by red, it may appear slightly green, and surrounding a grey with a bright color on the other hand may influence the eye to discern in the graying of the complementary of the bright colors.

Colors are most powerful on influencing the human mind and body. It is also the least expensive, easiest and quickest to use, to change or to create a decorating scheme. Colors can change the visual size and shape of a room as well as create an atmosphere and add warmth, vitality and beauty to room. Blue light has the shorter wavelength of about 470 nm than that of red having about 670nm. Longest wavelength is infra-red and the shortest is the ultra-violet.

The variations of different wavelengths of VIBGYOR are violet 400-450 nm; indigo-430-450 nm; blue 450-500 nm; green 500-570nm; yellow 570-590nm; orange 590-620 nm; and red 620-700 nm. We get such photograph of a spectrum of seven colors known as VIBGYOR, showing the shades of light ranging from 400 nm to 700 nm in wavelength.

Infra-Red
Red
Orange
Yellow
Green

One must always bear in mind that no individual is completely white (good) or black (bad), but is an amalgam of the tow "grey".

A sensible good blending can create a forceful creation.

The ancient Indian thinkers had rightly recognized the equality of the male and female forces, their need for each other for a harmonious co-existence and their coming together as equal partners in the process of creation. All the living creatures in the world are believed to be the children of natural, and the nature gives multi-million colors. **A good healthy nation is only possible when we are surrounded by a proper color and light arrangement. In darkness, there is only one color, i.e., black.**

17

Colors for Eight Directions as per Vastu Shastra

Colors for the Eight Directions

Vastu is based on the eight directions having individual deities, planets and its own colors as given below:

North: Belongs to the God KUBER, who has a store of wealth and prosperity. It is represented by the planet Mercury (Budh) and the color is Green.

East: Belongs to The God INDRA who gives us life, wealth and prosperity. It is represented by the Planet Sun (Surya) and the color is orange.

West: Belongs to The God VARUN who wields power over rain and water. It is represented by Saturn (Shani) and the color is navy blue.

South: Belongs to The God YAMA who has power over justice and death. It is represented by the planet Mars (Mangal) and the color is red.

North–East: Belongs to All Gods and Goddesses who rule this direction and it is the most auspicious corner. The North–East is represented by the planet Jupiter (Guru) and the color is yellow.

South–East: Belongs to The God Fire (Agni). It is represented by the planet Venus (Shukra) and the color is white.

South–West: Belongs to the Demoness, Nairuti (Putna). It is therefore, banned for all auspicious functions. It is represented by the Planet Dragon Head/Tail (Rahu/Ketu) and the color is grey/brownish with a red tint.

North-West: Belongs to Vayu Devta (The God of Wind). It is represented by the planet Moon (Chandra) and the color is pearl yellow.

18

Your Favorite Rashi Colors

Rashi Colors

Your favorite colors can be chosen based on the following colors suitable for each Rashi:

	Rashi	Sun Sign	Favourable Colors
1.	Mesh	Aries	All shades of red and yellow
2.	Vrishabh	Taurus	All shades of white and lighter shades of yellow
3.	Mithun	Gemini	All shades of green and red
4.	Kark	Cancer	All shades of yellow and orange
5.	Singh	Leo	Orange, deep red and white
6.	Kanya	Virgo	All shades of green and yellow
7.	Tula	Libra	Black and lighter yellow shades
8.	Vrishcika	Scorpio	All shades of deep yellow, red and blue
9.	Dhanu	Sagittarius	Yellow and lighter shades of blue
10.	Makar	Capricorn	Blue, violet and deep shades of yellow
11.	Kumbh	Aquarius	All shades of blue, copper and yellow
12.	Meen	Pisces	Blue and light shades of yellow

19

The Constitution of Most Widely Used Colors

Colors Most Widely Used:

Red: The most dramatic and emotional of all colors. The use of red suggests a bold and confident attitude, and is best used in areas that speak of excitement and vivaciousness.

Blue: The only color that is linked universally to tranquility and calmness. It is often best suited for a bathroom, where one tends to spend much time either in the shower or on the pot which is also a time to relax, and often, to think.

Yellow: A powerful color, not only in its hue, but also in its effect. It evokes a sense of energy and vitality, and rightly so, in places like the children's room, an art studio, classroom, chamber or a gym.

Green: Represents healing and fertility. Though not very commonly used in residences, it is the perfect color for new age healing centres, or the meditation room in the house.

Violet: The color or femininity and emotion; romance and fantasy. Violet on your bedroom walls ensures a good love life and heavenly dreams.

Orange: An amazingly versatile color that represents warmth, comfort and reassurance. Never really used in its true Saffron Orange hue, the pastel version or peach hue is quite popular for its cool effect on the ambience of a bedroom or study.

20

Energies From Colors and Light (Influencing the Mind, Body and Environment Around us)

The Environment Around us

Colors and light are very powerful in influencing the human mind and body. It is also the least expensive, easiest and quickest to use, to change or to create a decorating scheme. Colors and light can change the visual size and shape of a room as well as create an atmosphere and add warmth, vitality and beauty to a room and change the mood of the user.

During the Vedic Period, all colors were extracted from vegetables and flowers. These colors were more permanent in shade, soothing to the eye and had a natural tint. Even now in many parts of the world, instead of using synthetic colors, vegetable colors are used, particularly in textile printing and making designs, miniature paintings, ceramics, etc. Vegetable colors have no side effect on the skin and eyes.

During the Ice age, the bodies of dead persons were painted red or they painted their bones with red colors. Accordingly, the flow of red blood means the difference between life and death. They probably believed that the color itself was life giving.

The Egyptians used colors obtained from metal found in the Earth, plants, insects and fishes.

The symbolic use of color was made at a very early period in human history. During the early period, the heart which was the seat of life, and blood; both red in color, were identified with life and consciousness.

Yellow was possibly the color of fire and white depicted day.

If a room has poor daylight, it should be painted in light colors and if a room gets a good amount of natural light throughout the day, it can be painted in some deep colors. If a room has a window only towards the North that admits cold light, we should not use blue on the walls.

If a room gets plenty of direct sunlight, it is not advisable to paint the walls yellow and peach. It is always better to have the ceiling in white because a white ceiling reflects light into a room. It is also very important that the temperature of the ceiling is less than the temperature of the human body in order to have a healthy room.

A fluorescent tube light during the day or white color is harmful for human skin. It also changes the original tint of other colors.

Some colored lamps and shades produce curious effects. A person's face appears ghastly when seen by light passing through a blue shade, since there is an absence of red and warm tints that produce the normal healthy appearance of the face.

A red carpet will reflect more red rays by artificial light and will appear to be of a stronger red at night than during the day, but a blue carpet is a more intense blue in daytime than in the night. Purple color contains both, red and blue.

Color contrast in value is perhaps the most important factor in the composition of a design. Maximum contrast is obtained by the use of colors of extremely strong chromes.

A strong yellow on a black field is an excellent example of maximum visibility. A bright strong yellowish red would be considered as a powerful color. The color of an object depends upon the light it emits or sends back to the eye. Opposite contrast colors are quickly changed when mixed, as for black who makes colors both brighter and lighter in looks.

Surrounding an intense color with grey increases the apparent colorfulness of intense color making. It appears even brighter or more brilliant. Surrounded by yellow, a grey color may appear slightly blue. When surrounded by red, it may appear slightly greenish. On the other hand, a grey surrounded by a bright color may influence the eye to discern in the graying of the complimentary of the bright colors.

One must always bear in mind that no individual is completely white (Purity, Good) or black (Bad), but is an amalgam of the two 'Gray'. A good, sensible blending can create a forceful impression.

Ancient Indian thinkers had rightly recognized the male and female forces, their need for each other for a harmonious co–existence, and, their coming together as equal partners in the process of creation.

All living creatures in the world are believed to be the children of nature, and nature gives multi million colors. A good healthy nation is only possible when we are surrounded by proper color and light arrangements. In darkness there is only one color i.e. black. Therefore, blending of proper light (Daylight or artificial light) with recommended colors is very important.

The white color depicts day and is opposite to black. It is symbolic with night and death. Right from the past, even today, there has been continuity in the symbolic use of color. We associate red with parades and games, blue with that of outstanding work, purple as of dignity and reverence, green with nature and healing, yellow with sunshine and, of course, pink to good health.

21

Rhythm of Life with Changing Colors (A Scientific Discovery, Vastu Vedic Architecture)

From Sunrise to Sunset, environmental color changes correspondingly affect all living things. The very first sunrise to the sunset of the present, we continued to be awed by the beauty, power, life creating and life sustaining properties emanating from light.

It would therefore, appear that our physiological and emotional centers are synchronized with nature by way of light and that we truly seem to be the offspring of nature. Based on the awareness that daily color variations in the environment are intimately connected to the body's daily rhythmic changes. Humans have recognized that the seasonal color changes also reflect biological alterations within all living things.

Harmony within our life processes is related to the level of communication between our body and the environment. Imbalanced responses to specific rhythms, seasons and their associated cycles are related to specific kinds of physical and emotional problems.

Longevity may be related to our ability to integrate and synchronize ourselves with the planetary and solar – stellar energies that surround us. In humans, exposure to sunlight significantly influences physiological and psychological functions. Among these, fertility and mood are two of the most profoundly affected.

Light has played a consistent role in the development of all living things. More recently, Albert Szent Gyorgyi, Nobel Prize winner and the discoverer of Vitamin C, has recognized how profoundly color and light affect us. From his work, he concluded: "All the energy which we take into our bodies is derived from the sun." He saw that, through the process of photosynthesis, the sun's energy is stored in plants, which are in turn eaten by animals and humans take in the oxygen released.

The Sun is a source of mental energy. The best minds evolved in a natural process where the sun was temperate; not very hot, not very cold; just the right temperature (+ or – 3 degrees) of 24 degrees Celsius. The hot sun has glare, sharp light and dark shadows. The Cool sun has colors and rarely rises above the horizon or often geographically couples with heavy clouds in the sky and snow on earth. It is generally gloomy, but beautiful, with silvery and long hours of twilight.

Hot and humid zones with heavy cloudy sky for long periods of the year also have a distinctive culture and Architecture. The Sun has played an important role in the development of visual qualities of Architecture in terms of textures, color, roof forms and, above all, in every expression of vitality.

Science Discovers

The human body is nourished directly by the stimulation of sunlight; or nourished directly by eating foods, drinking fluids or breathing air that has been vitalized by the sun's light energy. Dr. Zame Kime, in his book "Sunlight", states that a series of exposures to sunlight will decrease the resting heart rate, blood pressure, rate of respiration, blood sugar and lactic acid in the blood following exercise. It also increases energy, strength, endurance, tolerance to stress and ability of the blood to absorb and carry oxygen. The human body is truly a living photocell that is energized by the sun's light; the nutrient of humankind.

Szent Gyorgyi discovered that many enzymes and hormones involved in processing this energy are colored and very sensitive to light. He added that light striking the body could literally alter the basic biological functions involved in processing the body's fuel that powers our lives.

In 1979, Martinek and Brezin found that:-

- Colors of light can stimulate certain bodily enzymes to be 500% more effective.
- Some colors can increase the rate of enzymatic reactions and activate or deactivate certain enzymes. Light not only affects us but our state of consciousness also determines how we use light.

Sunlight for Our Health

Sunlight has been used by all the major historical cultures and it has touched the hearts and creative minds of those who have learned to appreciate its potential. It wasn't until the 1800s that physicians throughout the world became fully aware of the healing properties of sunlight.

At this point in time, cures using light were being claimed for conditions ranging from simple inflammation and paralysis to tuberculosis. It was later discovered that sunlight striking the skin initiated a series of reactions in the body leading to the production of Vitamin D, a necessary ingredient for the absorption of calcium and other minerals from the diet. If Vitamin D is absent, the body will not absorb the amount of calcium required for normal growth and development of bones.

In 1903 Niels Finsen of Denmark was awarded the Nobel Prize for being the first person to successfully treat skin tuberculosis with ultra violet light. During his many years of work with both sunlight and ultra violet light, Finsen reported miraculous cures in thousands of patients.

The cosmic cycles affect our universe, which in turn affects the Solar System, which then affects the Earth and so on down through the Earth's Climate, seasons and inhabitants, right down to the smallest particle within an atom.

Since all things are integrally connected in this way, everything affects everything else. Nothing escapes this process. Universally occurring variation affects all living things.

Nature has a master plan for us to spend part of our lives exploring our external environments and part of our lives exploring our internal environments.

What the Vedas Say

It is very important to discuss and discover the indoor environment, particularly in the 21st Century, where the environment throughout the world is becoming more and more polluted, in relation to our health, productivity, universal peace and well being in general.

Most of the modern generation spends their working hours indoor, thus eliminating the morning sunlight and fresh air from their daily diets. The absence or imbalance of certain naturally present spectral light components causes a reduction in our physiological, emotional and intellectual functioning. Light, therefore, plays an integral role in the proper biological functioning of all living organism.

In this regard, Vastu play a very important role in helping in creating a clean environment, free from pollution of any kind, full of light and color needed for the development of a healthy nation with a peaceful environment by balancing the Five Elements of Nature.

Sanskrit Shloka:

Veda Says:-

Om Dyauh Shanti Antakrish Shanti Prithvi Shantiraapah
Shantiroshadhayah Shantih II
Vanespatayah Shantihvishvedavah Shantihr Brahma
Shantih Servagyum Shanti Shanti Revah, Shanti Sa Ma,
Shantiredhih, Om Shanti Shanti Shanti Om II

Sanskrit Shloka:

Na Pranena Na Apranena Matyo Jivati Kaschana I
Itarena Tu Jivanti Yasmin Etavapsritau II

Meaning:

Our life doesn't depend merely on the breathing process. The intake of diet is indeed important for health, but health does not rest on food alone, because everything can be thrown out of order if the mind is upset. A turbulence injected into the mind is enough to disturb the entire balance of personality. Your strength is in you. Religion begins where science ends; the beginning of the higher wisdom.

Radiant Energy

Ancient civilizations were apparently aware of light, namely, its route of entry into the body and some of its major effects on the body's regulatory centers and their functions. Major control centers of the body are directly stimulated and regulated by light, to an extent far beyond which modern science, until recently, has been willing to accept.

Though the body's balance is regulated by the autonomic nervous system, which is regulated by the very important part of the brain, the hypothalamus, which receives light energy through eyes, coordinates and regulates most of our life sustaining functions and also initiates and directs our reactions and adaptation to stress.

Many of us spend our lifetime chasing mental images rather than observing the realities of life. The general lack of awareness has already led to the toxification of life's most important basic elements: light, air, food and water.

Light is the major nutrient sustaining all life and it follows that poor and/or incomplete lighting will significantly affect every aspect of human existence. It is important to initially look at the constituents of sunlight as well as the kinds of artificial light to which we are exposed in our daily lives.

Light is composed of waves of radiant energy. Sunlight, which contains all the different wavelengths, provides the total electromagnetic spectrum under which all life on this planet has evolved.

Until 1879, when Edison perfected the light bulb, people spent most of their time outdoors and received adequate daily doses of natural full spectrum sunlight. The light bulb became largely an "indoor event", which drastically reduced the amount of time to which people exposed themselves to full spectrum sunlight.

Since most of us spend our working hours indoors, eliminating sunlight from our daily diets, it is important to find this indoor environment in relation to our health, productivity and in general.

22

Sunlight for Efficient Building Design

Energy from sunlight

1. The sun has abundant energy to make life comfortable and prosper on this planet Earth.
2. Energy from the nature is the base of Vastu Science. The whole Universe is a dynamic whole Web of energy pattern. Duration of time for exhausting of Earth Energy resources is as shown in Diagram -1

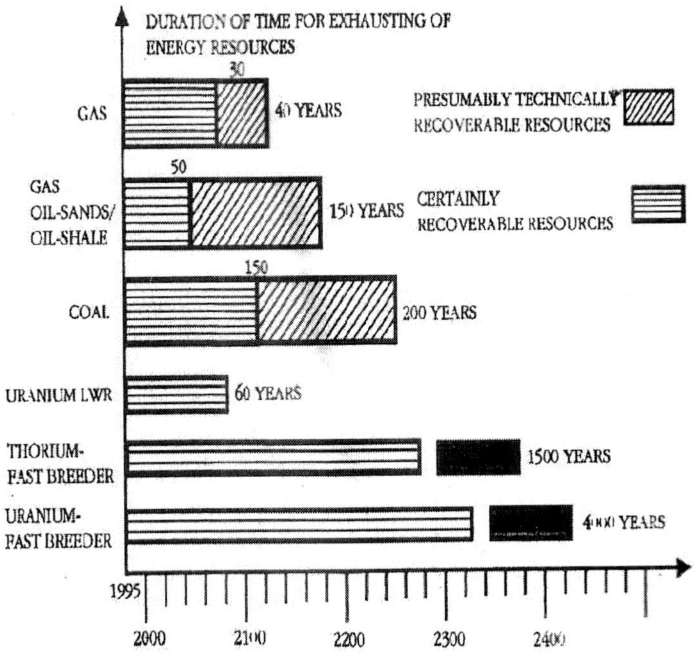

Diagram 1

3. Human beings get 99% energy from Sun which is the rhythm of daily life in the form of warmth and light for all actions/ reactions for all the life forms of Universe. Vastu consultant and architecture therefore, has to conserve energy with climatologically response for the overall growth of the inmates living/working in the built space. We have to learn to handle the delicate balance and sensitivities of natural energy, especially the Sun in design process so as to produce an environment full of energy.

Life on Earth is under the constant influence of natural sunlight. The worlds have always recognized connection with sunlight. It was profoundly recognized by the ancient cultures that they revered the Sun as God for its blessing.

Sustainer of Healthy Life

Sunlight containing Ultraviolet Rays (Invisible form of light) is beneficial to humans, and there are certain adverse effects too. Let us not say that the God may have made mistake in giving harmful Ultraviolet Light and Rays.

It is a misconception that 'nature' is hostile to man. If approached in true harmony, its secrets can be revealed and its energies harnessed for the benefit of the living. Nature, man and product are within evolutionary network guided by performance standards. Architectural beauty is to be seen, felt, perceived, conceived and experienced, the so-called 'moderns' are looking to the orient for the desired peace of mind. India is the source; the fountain-head of the vast ancient Vedic knowledge available on the planet. This open secret is relatively unknown: when the Vedic concept is presented through modern high-tech and technological advances, the sublime information becomes available and can be easily understood. This would give a new outlook in the world of architecture, art and sciences in 21st Century.

In the Vedic period, people built homes, temples, and hermitages, applying Vastu principles balancing the five elements with a view to having a peaceful living, offering prayers and to live in common harmony. But in the modern world people built concrete clusters, mainly for a high rate of return. After the Second World War, the architectural practice has turned into a race towards the so-called modernization. Adopting bureaucratic values that have resulted in worldwide pollution, environmental and ecological problems; with no peace of mind whatsoever under any kind of shelter.

Spectrum of the Sun

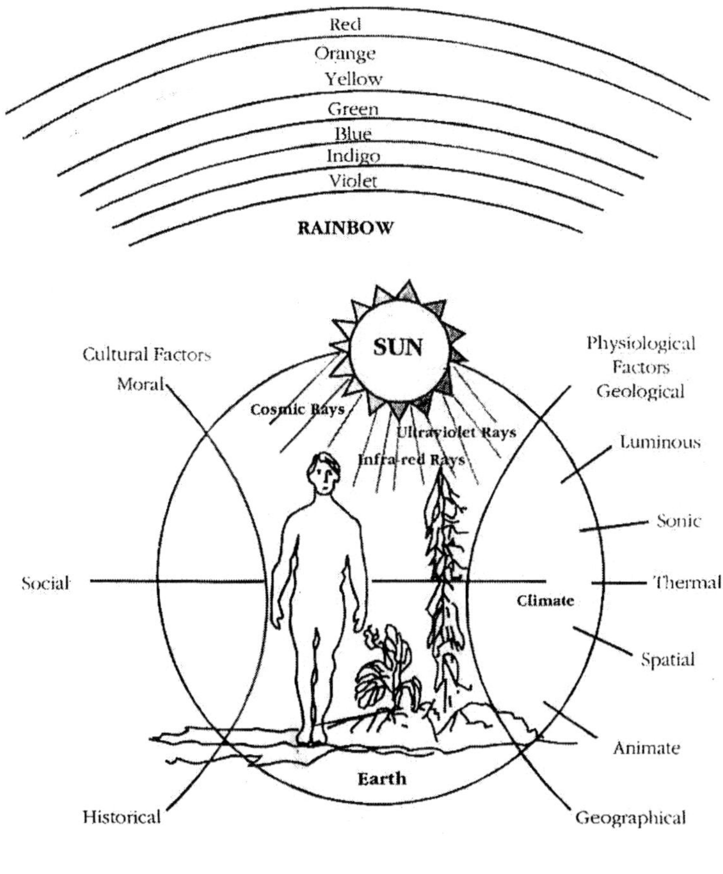

Human Comfort Level
Diagram 2

Ultraviolet (UV) Light

Ultraviolet light is an effective treatment for many diseases. The Sun Therapy is very commonly used as Naturopathy which includes treatment of anemia, gouts, colitis, cystitis, and arteriosclerosis, rheumatoid arthritis, eczema, acne, herpes, lupus, sciatica, asthma, kidney problems and even burns. People will have to understand that there are lots of health benefits from ultraviolet light as enumerated below:

1. UV Light increases the efficiency of heart. At the Tulane school of Medicine, Dr. Raymond Johnson exposed 20 people to Ultraviolet light. In 18 of out of 20 people their cardiac output increased an average of 39 percent! In other words, their hearts became stronger and pumped more blood.
2. UV Light reduces cholesterol. In one experiment, patients with hypertension and related circulatory problems were exposed to UV Light. Two hours after the first exposure, 97 percent of the patients had almost a 13 percent decrease in serum Cholesterol levels.
3. UV Light is an effective treatment for psoriasis. Reports from.

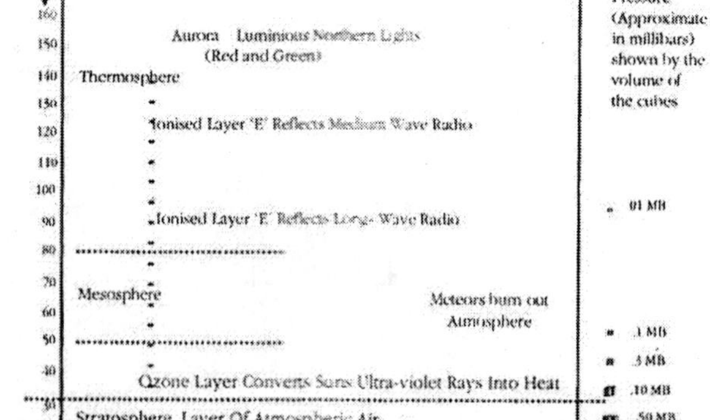

Diagram 3

Ozone Layer is a form of oxygen which protects us from most of the sun's ultraviolet radiation.

Solar energy that reaches our planet is affected in many ways by the atmosphere, those envelopes the land and water surface.

The National Psoriasis Foundation indicates that 80 percent of those suffering from this skin disease improve when they are exposed to UV Light.

4. UV Light activates the synthesis of Vitamin D, which is a prerequisite for the absorption of calcium and other minerals from the diet. Robert Neer and Associates conducted a study on a group of elderly persons to determine if extra sunlight would increase their ability to absorb calcium from their diets. The group which did not receive UV rays had 25 percent decrease in Calcium absorption while the other group receiving UV Rays had a 15 percent increase in absorption.
5. UV Light increases the level of sec hormones. In a study at Boston State Hospital, Dr. Abraham Myerson found that ultraviolet light increased male hormones level by 120 percent. UV Light activates an important skin hormone.
6. UV Light is an effective treatment for many diseases indicated above. UV Light has been found very effective in killing infectious bacteria, including several forms of tuberculosis bacteria.

Today, practically all sources of ultraviolet exposure are seen as detrimental to humans. It is well-known that tuberculosis was one of the main diseases that were treated by sunshine and many patients were completely cured.

It is very important to know and study in deep the UV Light and Infra-red rays, which we have discussed in next chapter, but first we must know that too much UV light is bad, "we need a basic amount to support life and maintain a healthy immune system." If someone says that oxygen is hazardous to our health we will say he does not understand gift of nature. Similar is conclusion for Ultraviolet, light.

Since sunlight (containing UV) is beneficial to humans and that there are certain adverse effects on persons living and working in artificial lighting. The light in most houses looks yellowish and dingy. The wavelength of light in the orange-pink-red range caused laboratory animals to lose their hair, show excessive calcium deposits in their hearts and develop large fast growing tumors. It was also found that when animal's cells were exposed to red and infra-red portions of the spectrum, their cell walls ruptured and cell division process (mitosis) stopped. Sunlight consists of a fairly balanced spectrum of color. Interestingly enough, blue is the wavelength most lacking in incandescent light bulbs. It has been established that ultraviolet light is a nutrient, just like a vitamin or a mineral. Daily allowance for UV light has, therefore, recommended just as in case of vitamin C.

In fact, overexposure to the sun, in conjunction with certain skin types, is a major factor in the development of skin cancer. The solution is quite simple, mild, sensible exposure to sunlight is not only safe, it is desirable. One of the constituent of sunlight is "ultraviolet" (UV) rays for which modern science has made us to think that it causes cancer, cataracts, aging and wrinkles. This blocking of ultraviolet rays may severely weaken the body's deafness.

What does nature say about solar light? The researchers have to understand the fact that human have evolved under nature sunlight. Are we supposed to dismiss five million years of evolution because science doesn't understand the supreme wisdom of nature?

According to photo biologist Dr. John Ott, there are strong indications the UV light through eyes stimulates the immune system. UV light in large amount is harmful; however in trace amounts, UV rays in nature sunlight, it acts, as a "life-supporting nutrient" which is highly beneficial.

Sunlight contains different ultraviolet (UV) radiation. UV light in classified as UV-A, UV-B, or UV-C depending on its wavelength. UV-A (320-380NM), directly adjoining the violet end of the visible-light spectrum is responsible for the tanning response in humans. UV-B (290-320 NM) activates th4e synthesis of vitamin D and the absorption of calcium and other minerals. UV-C (100-290 NM).

What are Ultraviolet Rays?

Ultraviolet rays are an invisible form of light. They lie just beyond the violet end of the visible spectrum. The sun is the major nature source of ultraviolet rays. Lighting, or any other electrical spark in the air, also emits ultraviolet rays. The rays can be produced artificially by passing an electric current through a gas or vapor, such as mercury vapor. Ultraviolet rays can cause sunburn. Overexposures to these rays can cause skin cancer. Ultraviolet rays also destroy harmful organisms and have other useful effects.

Sunlight for Efficient Building Design

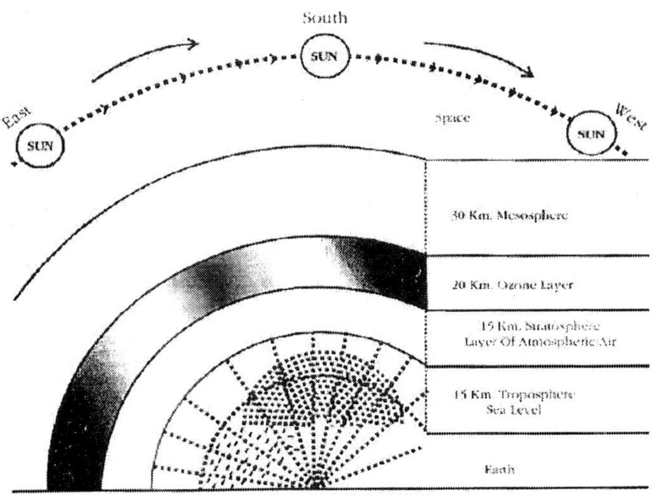

Diagram 4

Ultraviolet rays (UV) have shorter wavelength (WL) than visible light. A wavelength is the distance between the crests of two waves, is often measured in units called nanometer. One nanometer (MN) equals 0.000001 millimeter (0.000000039 inch.) wavelength of visible light range from about 400 to 700 nm. Ultraviolet wavelength range from about 1 to 400 nm. The wavelength of Ultraviolet rays determines whether a material they shine on absorbs the rays or transmits them.

For example, only ultraviolet rays with shorter wavelength can pass through ordinary window glass. The glass absorbs rays with shorter wavelength, though they can pass through other materials.

Uses of Ultraviolet Rays

Ultraviolet rays (UV) with wavelength (WL) shorter than 300 nm. Are effective in killing bacteria and viruses. Hospitals use germicidal lamps that produce these short rays to sterilize surgical instruments, water and the air in operating rooms. Many food and drug companies use germicidal lamps to disinfect various types of products and their containers. Direct exposure to ultraviolet rays with wavelengths shorter than 320 nm. Produces vitamin D in the body. Physicians once used sun lamps that produced these rays to prevent and treat rickets; bone diseases caused by the lack of Vitamin D. The lamps are used today to treat some skin disorders, such acne and psoriasis. Some instruments use ultraviolet rays to identify the chemical composition of unknown material. Medical researchers use such instruments to analyze substances in the human body, including amino acids, enzymes, and other proteins. The electronics industry uses ultraviolet rays in manufacturing integrated circuits.

Harmful Effects

The sun's shortest ultraviolet rays those with wavelength below about 320 nm. Are particularly harmful to living things.

Too much exposure to these rays can cause painful eye irritation or eye inflammation. High quality sun glasses protect the eyes from these rays. Overexposure to ultraviolet rays also can cause a painful burn. Melanin, a brown pigment in the skin, provides some protection against sunburn. Sunscreen lotion absorbs the sun's burning rays.

Exposure to the sun ultraviolet rays over a long period can cause skin cancer and other changes in human cells. Such exposure can also damage or kill plants. Ozone, a form of oxygen in earth's upper atmosphere, absorbs most of the sun's ultraviolet radiation. Without the ozone layer, ultraviolet rays would probably destroy most plant and animal life.

Scientific Research

Ultraviolet rays originate within the atoms of the elements. Scientists learn about the make-up and energy levels of atoms by studying the rays. Experts also learn about distant stars and galaxies by analyzing the ultraviolet rays that they give off.

Much research has focused on the role of ultraviolet rays in chemical reactions that break down the earth's protective ozone layer. As the ozone layer breaks down it becomes less effective as a barrier against harmful ultraviolet rays.

Example, only ultraviolet rays with shorter wavelengths can pass through ordinary window glass. The glass absorbs rays with shorter wavelength, though they can pass through other materials.

Experiments indicate that bees, butterflies, and other insects can see ultraviolet light. The reflection of ultraviolet rays of wings reveals patterns that help insects identify mates.

What is Ozone?

Ozone, OH zohn, is a form of oxygen that is present in the earth's atmosphere n small amounts. Ozone in the upper atmosphere is a major factor in making life on the earth possible. But ozone in the lower atmosphere contributes to air pollution. Ozone is used commercially in water purification processes and as a bleaching agent.

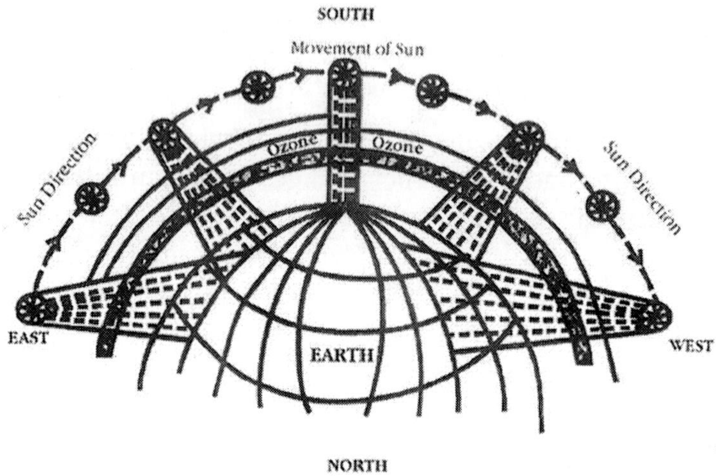

Diagram 5

Ordinary oxygen molecules have two oxygen atoms. Ozone molecules contain three oxygen atoms. Ozone is produced naturally through photochemical and electric discharge reactions. Photochemical production occurs when high energy radiation from the sun strikes ordinary oxygen in the earth's upper atmosphere and converts some of it to ozone. Electric discharge reactions, including lightning and electric sparks from motors, also converts some oxygen to ozone. Ozone is produced commercially by electric discharge in a machine called ozonizer.

Most zones are found in the upper atmosphere. The biggest concentration is reached, depending on the latitude, between 14 and 19 miles (23 and 30km.) above the earth's surface. This concentration is 10 parts per million by volume-that is 10 parts ozone per 1 million parts air. The ozone layer in the upper atmosphere shields the earth from 95 to 99 percent of the sun's ultraviolet rays. Overexposure to these rays is a leading cause of skin cancer as explained earlier.

In the early 1970's, some scientists expressed concern that chemical compounds called chloro-fluoro-carbons (CFCs) were breaking down the protective ozone layer. At that time, CFCs were widely used as propellants in aerosol spray cans. After CFCs are released, they slowly rise in to the atmosphere. When they reach the upper atmosphere, the sun's ultraviolet radiation breaks them apart. Some of the molecular fragments that result react with ozone, thereby reducing the amount of it.

In 1978, the United States Government banned fluorocarbon aerosols for most uses. However, the ban did not affect the use of CFCs as refrigerants or in insulation. Scientists reported early in 1988 that the ozone layer above Antarctica was disappearing at a faster rate than expected. In 1989, an international treaty limited the production of CFC by several major producers of these chemicals.

Most ozone in the lower atmosphere is considered an air pollutant. It is formed by chemical reactions between sunlight and pollutants already in the atmosphere. Ozone produced in this manner is a component of photochemical smog. Such ozone can directly damage rubber, plastic, and plant and animal tissue. It may undergo further chemical reactions that produce other damaging chemicals.

Exposure to certain concentrations causes headaches, burning eyes, and irritation of the respiratory tract in many individuals.

Ozone has the chemical formula O_3 and a molecular weight of 47.998. Pure ozone is a pale blue gas. It was first detected by means of its sharp, irritating odor, which is often noticed near electrical switches and machinery. The German chemist Christian Friedrich Schonbein discovered ozone in 1840.

What are Infra-red Rays?

1. The sun's ultraviolet rays striking or falling on any object or human beings etc. on the Earth produce Infra-red rays

in relation to its temperature with surrounding temperature.

2. INFRA-RED RAYS: Infra-red rays are often called heat rays, resemble light rays, but they cannot be seen by the human eye. They behave similarly to light rays in both Reflection and Refraction. Any object such as building material, metal furniture and much more made out of conductor and less in insulation etc. gives off infra-red rays in relation to its temperature. As an object gets hotter, it gives off more and more infra-red rays. Such devices as the sniperscope, which was invented during World War II (1939-1945), can pick up infra-red rays from object that are warmer than their surroundings. In this way, these devices can "see" such objects in the dark or through fog.

3. Photographers use film that is sensitive to infra-red rays to take pictures in places where there is no visible light. Doctors use infra-red lamps to treat skin diseases and sore muscles. In these treatments, the infra-red rays pass through the patient's skin and produce heat when they strike the affected area.

4. Infra-red waves lie just beyond the red end of the visible light spectrum. Sir William Herschel, a British astronomer, discovered infra-red rays in 1800 by observing the effect of the heat they produced.

How to Use Ultraviolet Light for Perfect Health?

With the previous explanation we come to a conclusion that UV rays with WL 1 to 300 n.m. is harmful for human consumption and WL 320 n.m. produces Vitamin D in our body and about 320 to 400 is good for human consumption. Refer Diagram No. 6.

Now the early morning sun-rays reaches the Earth Surface, passes through Ozone with more area, though reaches the earth surface with lesser radiation and cover more earth surface.

Though the W/L during sun rise up to 2 hours is 320 to 400 n.m. Is good for human consumption and if it mixes with cold water it multiplies the vitamin capacity and is very good for human skin and eye as well as produces positive energy.

As sun rises it comes closer to the earth and distance of WL between the crusts comes closer much below 300 n.m. and between 10:00 a.m. to 4:00 p.m. becomes Infra-red rays. This scientific theory has been discovered much earlier by authors of Vastu and they suggested the placement of five elements and to balance this they recommended as below:

1. Spend at least one hour outdoors everyday without worrying of the weather. However, whatever is required to be done outdoors should not be done indoors. Taking a walk outdoors, breathe in nature and see its beauty. Avoid exposure between the hours of 8:00 a.m. to 5:00 p.m. and avoid directly looking into the sun as it will damage your eyes. While indoors, sit by an open window. This will provide you with the full visible spectrum of light including the UV and the view of the outdoors will be relaxing to both the eyes and mind like green garden etc.
2. Wear neutral grey color sunglasses.
3. For those who wear glasses ask the specialist about UV-transmitting lenses.
4. Don't use colored contact lenses, as it can cause many problems as sunglasses. As such use clear white contacts.
5. UV-Transmitting Plastic Windows should be considered instead of regular glass, on the south side of the building.
6. Avoid use of Suntan Lotions having PABA. The U.S. Food Drug Administration has concluded that fourteen out of seventeen Suntan Lotions containing PABA can be carcinogenic when used in the sun and can cause genetic damage to the DNA in the skin.

Exposure to Electromagnetic Waves and Electric Radiation

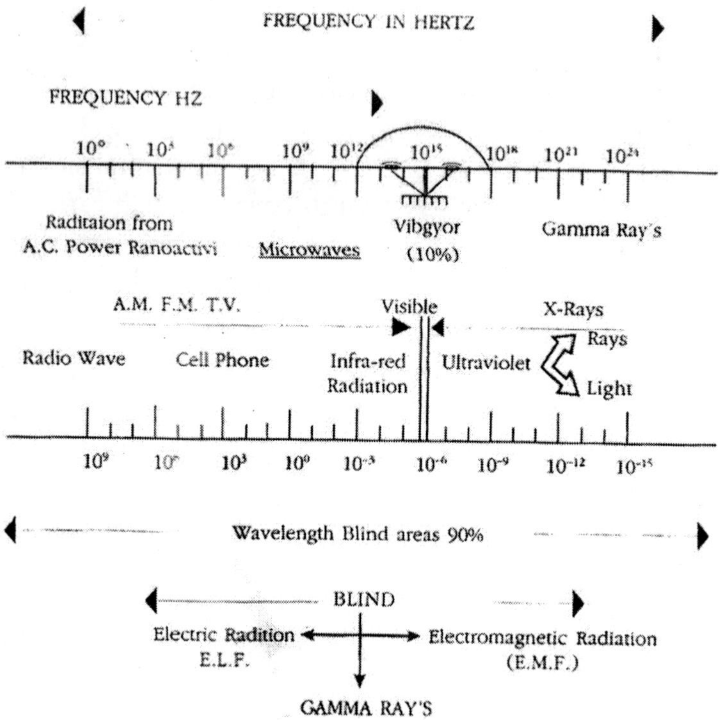

Diagram 6

Many people who work in areas where radiation may be present use an electroscope as a dosimeter. A Dosimeter is a device that measures the amount of radiation to which a person has been exposed. An electroscope must be charged before it can be used as a dosimeter. It gradually discharges when exposed to gamma rays, X-rays, or other forms of radiation. The amount of charge lost shows the level of exposure.

The first electroscope was made by William Gilbert, the physician of Queen Elizabeth I of England. He described it in a book published in 1600.

A dosimeter is a type of electroscope that measures the amount of radiation to which a person has been exposed. An X-rays technician wears a dosimeter that will change color if radiation is present.

The Sun's Electromagnetic Waves

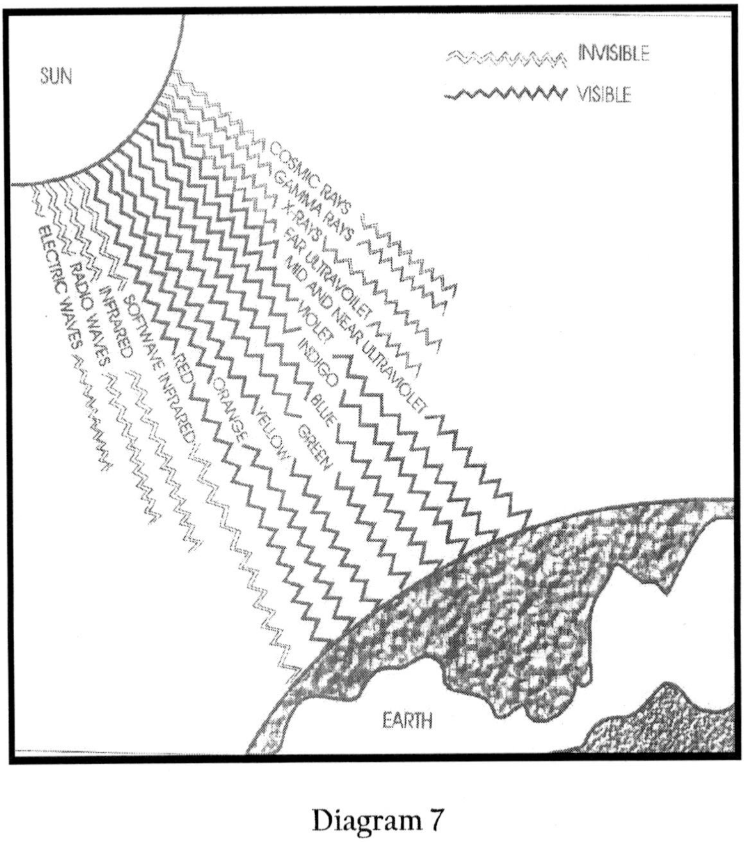

Diagram 7

Electromagnetic Waves

These are related patterns of electric and magnetic force. They are generated by the Oscillation (movement back and forth) of electric charges. Electromagnetic Waves travel through space at the speed of light- 186, 292 miles (299, 792 Kilometers) per second. The simplest electromagnetic waves are plane waves. They move through space in straight lines.

The strength of ht wave varies in space and time with alternating crests and troughs. The distance from crest-to-crest is called the wavelength.

The Electromagnetic Spectrum

It consists of bands of different wavelengths. The chief kinds of electromagnetic waves are in order of increasing wavelength-gamma rays, X-rays, ultraviolet light, visible light, infra-red rays, and microwaves and radio waves. Gamma rays are less than 10 trillionths of a meter in length, and some long radio waves measure more than 10,000 km.

All types of electromagnetic waves have the properties of visible light. They can be reflected, diffracted (spread), and refracted (bent). The direction of magnetic force in all electromagnetic waves is perpendicular to the direction in which the wave is moving. The direction of electric force is perpendicular to both the direction of magnetic force and the direction of wave motion. The strength of magnetic force always equals the strength of electric force.

The electromagnetic spectrum extends from short gamma rays through light waves to long radio waves. Thus, spectrum diagrammed below gives the frequency and wavelength for the various waves. Frequencies are given in hertz and wavelengths in meter. The raised figures with the 10's are a way of abbreviating numbers for example 10^{15} hertz equals 1 followed by 15 zeros, or 1, 000, 000, 000, 000, 000 hertz. The numbers with a minus sign tell how many places the decimal point must be moved in front of the number. For example, 10^{7} meters equals 0.0000001 meter.

Uses of Electromagnetic Waves

Doctors use gamma rays, which are given off by radium, to treat cancer. They also use X-rays to treat cancer and, in addition, to help, locate and diagnose internal disorders. Ultraviolet rays are used in Sun lamps and fluorescent light and as a disinfectant. Infra-red rays, which are given off by hot objects, are used in infra-red lamps to treat skin disease and to bake enamel. Micro waves ware used to cook food. Radio waves are used in radio and T.V. broadcasting.

The technological use of electromagnetic waves depends on the ease with which the various wavelengths can be dictated and produced. Wavelength is related to the vibration rate of electrons in the energy source. The slower the vibration, the longer the wavelength. Long waves are the easiest to produce, and the use of radio waves in communication begun soon after 1900.

Shorter waves were not effectively utilized until the development of such devices as the Klystron, a type of microwave tube. Development of the laser during the1960 provided new uses for short waves. For example, the laser enables ultraviolet and infra-red rays to transmit voice messages and television signals.

Electromagnetism

Electromagnetism is the branch of physics that studies the relationship between electricity and magnetism. Electromagnetism is based on the fact that (1) an electric current produces a magnetic field, and (2) a changing magnetic field produces an electric field.

In 1920s, the Danish scientist Hans Oersted discovered that a conductor carrying an electric current is surrounded by a magnetic field. When he brought a magnetized needle near a wire in which an electric current was following, the needle moved. Because a magnetized needle is moved by magnetic forces, the experiment demonstrated that an electric current produces magnetism.

During the 1820s the French physicist Andre Marie Ampere declared that electric current produces all magnetism. He concluded that a permanent bar magnet has tiny currents flowing in it. The work of Oersted and Ampere led to the development of the electromagnet, which is used in such devices as the telegraph and the electric current flows through the wire. If the direction of the current changes, the poles of the electromagnet switch places.

Magnetism produces an electric current by means of electromagnetic Induction. The English scientist Michael Faraday and the American physicist Joseph Henry discovered electromagnetic induction independently in 1831. In electromagnetic induction, a changing magnetic fields set up an electric field and within the conductor. For example, a magnet moving through a coil of wire causes the voltage to vary from point-to-point along the wire. An electric current flows along the wire as long as the amount of magnetism passing through the wire is changing. Electromagnetic induction is the basis of electric generator. An electric motor reverses the process. A current sent through the wire sets up a magnetic field, which causes the wire to move.

In 1864, James Clerk Maxwell, a British scientist, used the earlier experiment to show that electric and magnetic fields act together to produce radiant energy in the form of electromagnetic waves.

How to Use Ultraviolet Light and Infra-red Rays for Efficient Building Design Based on Vastu Principles

Solar Energy

Sun is the greatest source of energy. Nut its distribution on earth is unequal. Certain places get more of its heat and certain places comparatively less. Why is it so?

We know that our earth is spherical in shape and flat at the poles. The Sun's rays fall on different places of the earth's surface at different angles. On the Equator, they fall straight but on the North and the South of the equator they fall obliquely. Because of the straightness of the falling rays, it is very hot at the equator, but as we go away it becomes progressively colder towards the poles.

Naturally, the question arises, why the obliqueness of the rays does reduce the heating effects. This is so because the rays falling obliquely have to travel longer distances in the atmosphere. The dust particles vapour and other materials present in the atmosphere absorb much of the heat contained in these rays. Hence, the longer the distance travelled by the sun's rays, the lager is the absorption of the heat by the atmosphere. Therefore, areas receiving the sun's rays obliquely receive less heat.

Thus, the places on or around the equator are very hot because they receive the sun's rays straight. On the other hand, places to the North and the South of the Equator are cold because they receive Sun's rays obliquely. The hotness or coldness of a place also depends on the distribution of water, its height above the sea level and distance from the sea-shore.

Methods of Heat Transfer

There are three ways in which heat is transferred namely:

(a) Conduction, (b) Convection, and (c) Radiation

a) **Conduction:** Conduction is the process by which heat is transferred through matter from place of high temperature to that of low temperature, without transfer of matter itself. If one end of an iron rod is placed in fire, the other end gets heated by conduction.

b) **Convection:** In Convection, heat is carried from one place to another place by the bodily transfer of the matter contained in it. Fluids, whether liquids or gaseous, are generally heated by convection.

c) **Radiation:** Radiation is the process by which heat is transferred from one body to another without heating the intervening medium.

Out of these methods of heat transfer, radiation plays the most important part in the transfer of heat in the atmosphere. The sun is intensely hot, the temperature of its surface being estimated as 6000°C. About a half of the solar radiation heating the earth is reflected back to space. The atmosphere does not absorb any appreciable amount of the sun's radiation. It is only when the energy penetrates to the earth's surface that it is absorbed and tends to raise the temperature of the ground, in turn, warms the air-layers in contact thus, the air in the atmosphere is heated, not directly by the sun but indirectly by the earth.

Solar power can be harnessed only if sun's rays are concentrated by using a series of mirrors. Solar energy has been taped to generate electricity, heating homes, providing hot water and hot air for industries. Satellites and space stations tap solar energy. Solar energy can be tapped only during periods of sunshine. Widespread use of solar energy will depend on technological developments so as to reduce costs and enable storage of power for use during cloudy periods or night. The solar energy would then provide continuous supply of abundant power.

Radiation and Insulation

Radiation means movement of rays. The quantity of solar hear transmitted in one minute to one square cm. of the earth's surface normal to the sun's rays beyond the earth's atmosphere are defined as solar constant which is approximately 2 cal. Per sq. cm. per minute. One square meter of the sun's surface radiates energy presumably equal to 100,000 hp. At the velocity of light. This energy is transmitted as ultraviolet radiation (short waves) and infra-red radiation (long waves).most of these radiations are perceived as heat and only an insignificant part as visible light.

As is known, every in 24 hours the earth completes a radiation around its axis at a speed of 27 kilometers per minute. At the same time, the earth revolves around the sun on a slightly elliptical orbit at a speed of 28.7 kilometers per second the period of revolution is equal to 365 days.

The movement of the earth around the sun together with the inclination of its axis of rotation results in an uneven distribution of light and heat in the various regions of the earth for any given year.

The position of the earth during its revolution around the sun is measured by the angle of the sun's rays in relation to the equatorial plan of the earth. This angle is called the solar declination and varies between 23.5° North latitude and 23.5° South latitude. The days of the year when the solar declination reaches these values are called the equinoxes. In the period of solstices the perpendicular rays of the sun areas of the earth that are at the maximum distance to the North and South of the Equator. The boundaries of these areas are indicated by imaginary lines on the surface of the earth designating the Tropic of Cancer as the northern limit and the Tropic of Capricorn limit.

Passing through the atmosphere, the solar energy is dispersed and absorbed, thus greatly depleting the solar radiation of the earth. The thermal conditions of an urban environment are made up of direct solar irradiation (Insulation) and its derivatives, scattered and reflected radiation and ambient air temperature. In regions with hot climates, direct radiation and ambient air temperature. In regions with hot climates, direct radiation is factor exerting the greatest influence on urban environments. The action of direct radiation can be greatly moderated by urban planning methods such as water impounding, shading, special landscaping, etc.

With an increase in the elevation above sea level, the intensity of radiation increase on an average by 10 percent for each 300 meter above sea level.

In large towns and deserts where there is a high dust content in the air, depletion of the intensity of scattered radiation is as much as 30-45 percent of the total amount of solar energy reaching the earth, the atmosphere absorb 15 percent, consequently the depletion of solar radiation by dispersion and absorption for different latitudes of the earth varies greatly. It is primarily determined by the incident angle of the sun's rays. When the sun is at the Zenith, the rays, falling vertically, intersect the atmosphere by the shortest path. With a decrease in the incident angle the path of the sun's rays becomes longer and depletion of solar radiation becomes greater.

On the other hand, the surface of the earth has the property of reflecting heat in to space. Temperature conditions of sea and land are by no means identical; moreover the surface of the land is not heated uniformly since some places are steppe land, meadow and plough land, other places-forests and swamp lands, still other places – deserts which do not have a soil covering. Vegetative covering darkens the earth's surface thereby decreasing the flow of heat into the soil. At night, on the contrary, the vegetative covering protects the soil from heat loss. Besides, part of thermal energy is also expended on the transpiration of plants. As a result, soils covered with greenery receive less heat in the daytime. During the daytime, especially in summer, the surface of the ground becomes heated and at night is cooled. The difference between maximum and minimum temperatures is called the daily fluctuation amplitude.

As is known, the heat capacity of water is two times greater than the heat capacity of land which means that under the same conditions for a definite period of time the surface of the land receives twice as much heat, as the surface of water. Besides, when water is heated it evaporates thus, expending a considerable part of thermal energy. However, having a greater heat capacity, the sea accumulates more heat than land with the result that the surface for the sea is warmer than the surface of land. The mean temperature of the surface of sea and ocean exceeds the average air temperature of the planet by 3°C.

The annual air temperature cycle for various parts of the world varies greatly, and is largely determined by the latitude of the localities. Depending on latitude, there are four basic types of annual temperature cycles: equatorial, tropical, temperature and arctic.

Insulation is the direct solar irradiation on the earth's surface which exerts a thermal, light and biophysical effect on man's organism.

In this connection, an interesting proposal was made by architect K. Gutchov recommending a "solar hour" (direct solar radiation per hour) as a convenient unit of measurement in calculating insulation, which takes into account the varying intensity of solar illumination for various times of the day and year. However, only those hours are of value when the sun is at an altitude of not less than 6 degree above the horizon and the angle of its rays to the surface of wall and window is not less than 15 degree.

In the planning and construction of a town, its territory is divided so that buildings will alternate with open spaces (lawns, greenery and water basins). This stimulates the exchange of air and retards overheating. Temperature fluctuations are also caused by varying building densities and the character of the topography of the site.

With the aim of lowering the heat load, the building pattern should take into account the closely related problems of orientation, insulation, ventilation, and building heights and building density. When buildings are placed on the perimeter of super blocks, it is advisable that the orientation of the street network be agreed with the position of the sun. In that case, the necessary insulation of building will depend on the accepted width of streets, building heights and their location along the street line.

Spacing between the buildings should ensure required insulation. Spacing between buildings depends on how the buildings are placed with their main facades parallel to the street or perpendicular to it. In hot climates the spaces between the buildings should provide sufficient area for green space as a means of protection against reflected radiation. With these conditions in mind, it is inadvisable to place building directly on the street line.

Building density also affects the micro-climate in hot-humid and dry zones. In the humid pattern, in which groups of buildings shade each other, it improves the micro-climate. Thus, in the first instance, an open layout of buildings. On the site is advisable. A latitudinal position of the larger axis of a building with a deviation of up to 15 degree on both sides (for better insulation) is believed to be the4 best orientation for many hot countries. With minimum spacing, buildings will receive maximum mutual shading.

Playing an effective role in the depletion of solar radiation are green spaces. Depending on their density, radiation is decreased by as much as 86 percent compared with an open area. In a tropical climate, it is advisable to provide covered passageways for pedestrian traffic for protection against sun and rain.

Solar Architecture and Energy Conservation through Building Design

Today, the world finds itself in the grip of an energy crisis more particularly in the 21st century. The known sources of conventional energy are dwindling very fast. The demand for energy especially in the third world is growing. And their efforts for development are constantly being threatened by environmental issues. The development nations which are the largest consumers and producers of energy face biggest the crunch.

This has aroused an interest in the development of energy resources as well as conservation of the available sources. And a lot of research and thinking is being generated in this new field. Solar energy, biotechnology and superconductivity have the highest priorities in research fields.

We, in India, have very low energy consumption levels as compared to consumption in developed countries. However, much we may be wise to increase the production of conventional energy our efforts are going to face resistance. The Narmada project is a very good example of this. Hence, before achieving any increase in the consumption of energy, we have to start thinking of conserving the same.

This situation forces upon us the issues of conservation of energy techniques. We can learn from the developed nation's efforts in this sphere. It gives us a chance to reallocate our resources in better ways even before the energy situation becomes acute.

Building construction, building design and architecture are such fields where the studies and research in energy conservation and renewable energy can be applied innovatively and creatively.

Passive solar energy system collects transported heat by natural means. Passive systems are simple in concept and use. The most striking difference between passive and active system in that the former operates on the energy available in its immediate environment and the latter imports energy to make the system work.

Architecture in the twentieth century has been characterized by an emphasis on technology to the exclusion of other values. There is an increasing dependence on mechanical control of the indoor environment rather than exploitation of climatic and other nature processes to satisfy our comfort requirements. Little attention is paid to the unique character and variation of local climate, building materials as well as the result is the monotonous character of our buildings. Since the passive solar system uses its energy and material from local environment, this can result into an ambient architectural character. Since solar energy is conveniently distributed to all parts of the globe, expensive transportation and distribution networks of energy are also eliminated.

Application of passive solar energy has to be included in every step of building design whereas conventional cooling and heating system can be independent of the conceptual organization of a building. It is extremely difficult to add passive solar system to a building once it is constructed.

Building Location, Shape and Orientation

Building shapes without regard for the sun's impact require large amounts of energy to cool in summer or heat in winter in cold climates.

A building elongated along the East-West axis will expose more surface area to the south during the summer and collect solar radiation and heat. This elongated shape is the most efficient shape in all climates for minimizing cooling requirements in summer and heating requirements in winter. In hot climates, buildings oriented along the North-South axis pay a severe price in energy consumption for cooling.

Beside orientation and shape, each façade of building needs careful treatment so as to gain maximum advantages to heat, light and wind.

India is broadly divided into two climatic zones. One zone below 28° NL and one above the same. The first has hot climate while the northern zone is in cooler zone. Hence, treatment of South and North facades depends on the locations.

North Side Kuber: The North side of a building is the coolest and darkest side. In severe summer conditions, room on north side provides cool atmosphere while in severe cold they are very cold and uncomfortable and should be avoided at any cost. However, north side gives very comfortable day-light in the interiors as provided in the north light roof in factory buildings.

South Side Yama: A room on the south with large openings and glass areas will convert the room in a hot case which is comfortable in cold region while the same is to be completely avoided in hot and arid zones. A cavity wall on South side will help in keeping heat away from indoors while a heat storage wall with glass panel in the front can provide the necessary heat on the inside in cold climates. In both cases, careful treatment of south façade is important in reducing the mechanical cost of heating or cooling.

Inner Courtyard Brahma: It is our common experience that old, traditional houses in hot regions in India provide very comfortable, cool atmosphere inside the buildings. A great interest has been aroused in studying this phenomenon and careful location and proportion of inner courtyards help provide comfortable light and ventilation and have great significance in passive solar architecture.

Heat Strong Wall: In cold climates, as they are found in northern part of our country, heating of room is necessary. The southern side specially treated with "TROMBE WALL" construction or addition of a green house can naturally provide heating not only in daytime but also at night. While the same wall can help sun radiation and heat reaching on inside in summer.

Roof Shading: The roofs receive maximum radiation and heat from the sun in the daytime in the hot regions and make the interior very hot. The various methods of providing shading devices can be used to protect roof while in cold climates, the roof radiates heat from inside to the atmosphere, rendering the interiors very cold. Hence, insulation of roofs also very important. Water ponds over the roof have advantage in both the climates.

Earth Sheltered and Earth Bermed Structures

The Earth bermed structures are suitable for areas where solar heating and cooling are designed. In such structures, the reduced infiltration of air from outside and the thermal resistance of surrounding earth considerably reduce the average thermal load.

Ventilation and Cooling: Air vents and wind towers operate in various ways. They are useful in hot arid climates. Air in the upper part of the wind tower is cooled. Water is introduced in the system and evaporative cooling takes place. This involves a change in water-vapour content and air temperature. And this air is admitted at the lower level of the room which creates a comfortable atmosphere inside. Air vents are employed in areas where dusty winds make wind towers impractical.

East-West orientation, with courtyards in the main building, bermed earth construction, south facing solar panels for generating energy, north light and well-protected main entrance on North with shading devices, solar water distillation plans on roof etc. can be given.

The houses are designed around a courtyard with all the main activity areas facing the same. While the outer walls are earth bermed, the houses are taken below the ground level, the courtyard has platform for solar cookers. Solar water heaters are provided on the rooftops for hot water requirements of housing.

Sol-Air Approach: The "sol-air" approach to orientation recognized that air temperature and solar radiation act together to produce one sensation of heat in the human body. Thus, to utilize the sun's rays fully, their thermal impacts must be considered in conjunction with heat convection, and the total effect measured by its ability to maintain temperature levels near the "comfort zone."

The importance of the sun's heat will, then, vary according to regions and seasons. Under cold conditions its additional radiation will be welcome and a building should be positioned to receive as much radiation as possible, while under conditions of excessive heat, the orientation of the same building should decrease undesirable solar impacts. By means of the bio-climatic chart these two conditions can be defined as the under heated and overheated period of the year. An optimum orientation for a given site would give maximum radiation in the under heated period. Simultaneously, reducing insulation to a minimum in the overheated period.

The various in orientation produced by regional requirements is diagrammatically presented in the accompanying illustration. In northern latitudes, the air is generally cool and there is a great need for the sun's heat. Consequently, building should be oriented so as to receive the maximum amount of radiation throughout the year. However, the same building in the South, where the air is heavy with heat, should turn its axis to avoid the sun's unwanted radiation and pick up cooling breezes instead.

The effects of solar radiation upon various orientations are illustrated here by rotating a vertical surface around the compass at 30 degree intervals and calculating the resultant thermal impacts.

Solar Control

The age-old problems of controlling the reception of solar radiation in buildings have been sharply enlarged by the modern developments in architectural planning and construction. Traditional massive bearing-walls, which combined the function of support with protection from light and heat, have been supplanted by clear structural members devoted to load-bearing (the skeleton) and covered with curtain walls (the skin) made of many materials.

The skin of a building performs the role of a filter between indoor and outdoor conditions, to control the intake of air, heat, cold, light, sounds, and odours. It is generally agreed that air, temperature, wind, and sound are best controlled within the wall itself, while light is easier to control inside the building shell, and heat radiation is most efficiently halted before it reaches the building envelope proper.

The materials of a building skin play a decisive part in the utilization and control of solar rays. The first example is a full glass window wall. With its straight approach, appealing as it is, the wall has to absorb all the penalties of the environmental variations, since the bare glass pane offers very little (around 12 percent) protection form radiation.

A diametrically opposite example is the fully opaque curtain wall. In some cases this envelops a building totally, leaving the entirely independent interior free for man-made conditioning. No doubt this solution has its rightful place in specific and peculiar situations, but a fully engineered atmosphere divorced from nature leaves known psychological deficiencies and most probably has still undiscovered drawbacks.

The use of heat-intercepting glass permits the use of large window wall with less heat penetration than allowed by ordinary glass. A relatively light-colored heat-absorbing glass intercepts over 40 percent of the radiant energy. This is a considerable aid in summer cooling, but unfortunately it also represents a loss of useful heat in winter.

The last example illustrates a radiation control solution with shading device. The method is fundamentally sound. Interception of the energy happens at the right place-before it attacks the building. In this way the obstructed heat is reflected and can dissipate into the outside air. Shading device gives by far the most efficient performance, since by shaping them according to the changing seasonal sun-path; both summer shading and winter heat gain can be achieved.

Location, latitude, and orientation all contribute the formulation of an effective device. In addition, the sun breaker can express a strong spatial character, add new elements to the architectural vocabulary, and phrase a truly regional consciousness.

The material which provides a screen between man and the natural environment offer rich possibilities for visual expression. Many materials only elaborate the surface others invite a play of light and shadow or add to the spatial composition, while some constitute their own architectural entities. To their plastic appearance they add visual ties or rhythm, light, color, and texture.

To control heat entry-the first line of heat control lies at the surface. Since the surface temperature of a sunlit material will be higher than that of the air, air movement over an exposed surface will reduce the external heat impact and be particularly beneficial under hot conditions. The exchange effect can be increased by diluting the radiation over a larger area by means of curved surface (such as vaults and domes), or corrugated uneven surfaces (such as alternating recessed brick layers), which will also simultaneously increases the rate of convection transfer.

The selective absorptive and emissivity characteristics of materials are another very effective defence against radiation impacts and especially important in overheated conditions. Materials which reflect rather than absorb radiation and which more readily release the absorbed quantity as thermal radiation will cause lower temperatures within the structure.

The sun's energy, by the time it falls upon a building, has been cut down by the atmosphere and arrives through several different channels. The solar radiation consists of visible wavelengths (0.3 to 0.7 microns). Since this energy is concentrated near the visible part of the spectrum, the criterion of reflectivity is an approximate relation to color values. White materials may reflect 99 percent or more, black materials 15 percent or less, of the radiation received.

On the other hand, the thermal exchange with the surroundings consists of longer infra-red wavelengths (over 2.5 usually from 5 to 20 microns). This range can also be classified as 9 microns. The characteristics of materials in regards to reflectivity of long-wave infra-red heat depend more on the density of surface and on molecular composition than on color.

The summer rays of high elevation may be intercepted by building elements of high reflectivity. In zones where hot conditions prevail, the net effect of reflectivity combined with the emissive thermal radiation characteristic of the material has to be considered.

If surfaces exposed to the irradiation of the sun and to a clear sky are whitewashed, painted white or built of light-colored material such as marble, they will remain cooler than surface of polished metal such as aluminium. Despite the fact that aluminium has a higher reflectivity to solar radiation, the effect is outbalanced by the emissive capability of the white surface which loses heat by thermal radiation towards the sky. This principle accounts for the white exteriors of tropical buildings. However, if the same materials are exposed not only to the sun but t hot ground where the white surface is not capable of losing heat by emissivity, the polished aluminium will be the cooler of the two materials. The application of both processes is utilized by aeroplanes, where the upper part exposed to solar radiation is painted white, while the lower portion remains metallic.

By converting solar energy into heat, heating can be provided locally. The selection of color and materials can reduce the effect of solar heating to some extent. The greatest source of heat gain can be the solar radiation entering through a window. This could, in fact, increase in the indoor temperature far above the door temperature, even in moderate climates. Because once the radiant heat has entered through a window it is trapped inside the building.

The four methods to control solar heat gain through window are explained here.

1. **Orientation and Size of the Window:** In the equatorial location to avoid solar heat gain the main windows should face north or south. Monor opening of unimportant room should be placed on the East and West side. Solar heat gain on the West side can be particularly troublesome as its maximum intensity coincides with the hottest part of the day.

2. **Internal Blinds and Curtains:** They are not very effective ways to solar control but they do stop the passage of radiation, and they themselves absorb the solar heat and can reach a very high temperature.

3. **Special Glasses**

a) **Heat Absorbing Glasses:** Achieve a selection transmittance by selectivity in absorption they reduce substantially the infra-red transmission.

b) **Heat Reflecting Glasses:** Achieves a similar selective transmittance by selectivity in reflection. The glass is coated by a thin film of metal (nickel or gold) applied by vacuum evaporation. Such glasses absorb very little heat; therefore, the improvement in reducing the total solar gain is far greater.

c) **Light Sensitive Glasses:** (Photocromatic glasses) these contain submicroscopic halide crystals which turn dark when exposed to strong light and regain their transparency when the light source is removed.

d) **Shading Devices:** Three Different Types:

e) **Vertical Devices:** Course blades or projecting fins in a vertical position. This type of device is most effective when the sun is to one side of the elevations, such as an eastern or western elevation. A vertical device to be effective when the sun is opposite to the wall considered would have to give almost complete cover of the whole windows. (Vertical and Horizontal Suitable for South and West Angle Facing Sun.)

f) **Horizontal Devices:** May be canopies, horizontal Louvre blades or externally applied venetian blind. These will be most effective when the sun is opposite to the building face considered and at a high angle such as for North and South facing walls.

g) **Eggerate Devices:** They are combination of horizontal and vertical elements the many types of grille-blocks and decorative screens may fall into this category. These can be effective for any orientation depending on detail dimensions. Construction of a shading mask also comes under this category.

Views / *Plans & Section* / *Mask* / *Example*	*Characteristics*
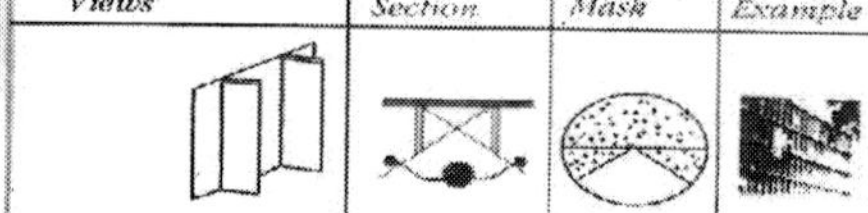	Vertical fins serve well towards East and West and need these orientations. There mask chae is segmental.
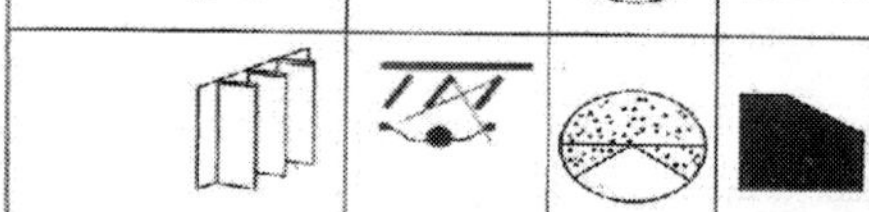	Vertical fins oblique to wall will result in asymetrical mask.
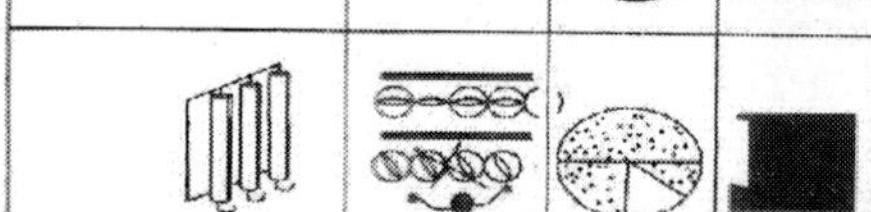	Movable fins can shade the whole wall or open up in different direction ACC. sun position.
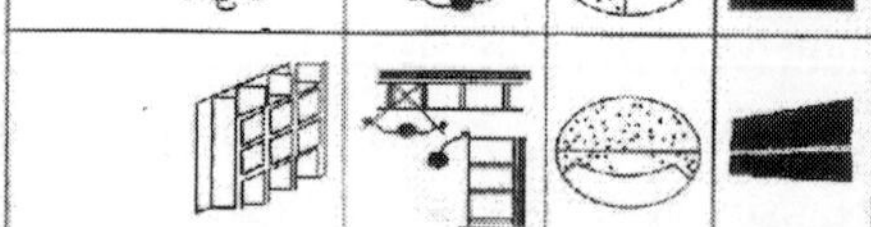	Eggerate types are the combinations of vertical and horizontal types and the mask is super imposed diagram of two masks.
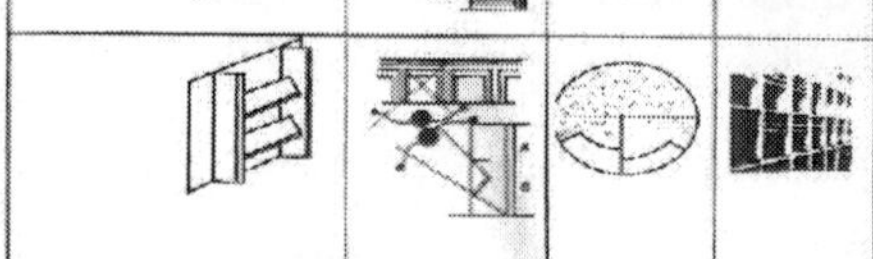	Eggerate devices with movable horizontal elements show flexible mask characteristics. They are efficient in hot due to high shading ratio.

Vertical and Eggerate Types of Shading Devices
Diagram 8

View	*Section*	*Mask*	*Example*	*Characteristics*
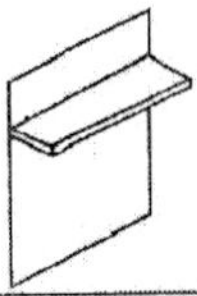	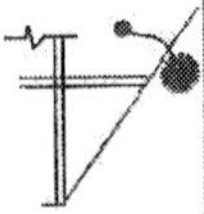	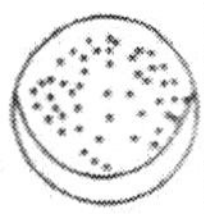	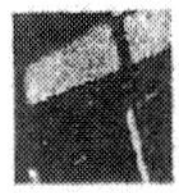	Horizontal Overhangs are most efficient towards South around Southern orientation. Their Mask Characteristic is segmental.
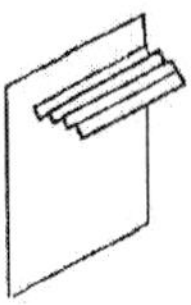	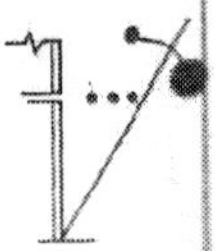	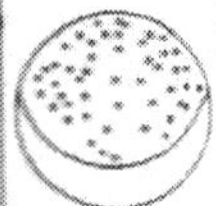		Louvre parallel to the wall have the advantage to permit air circulation near to the elevation. It gives better protection than vertical ones.
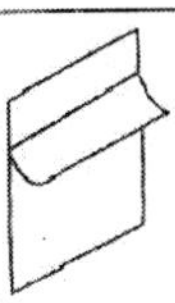	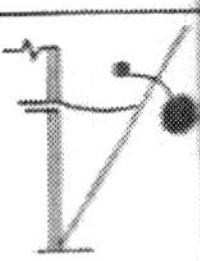	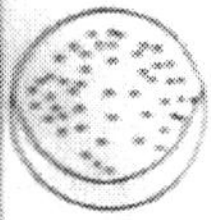		Canvas canopies will have the same characteristic as solid overhangs and can be made retractable.
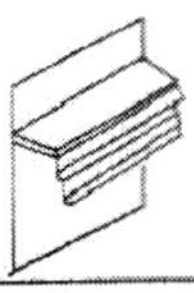		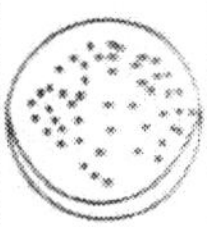		Where protection is needed for low sun angles, louvre hung from soild horizontal overhangs are efficient.
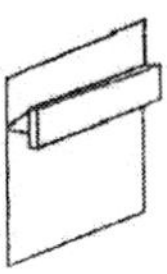	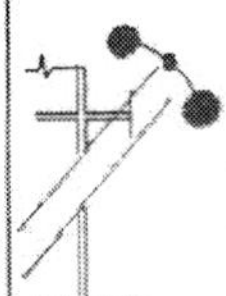	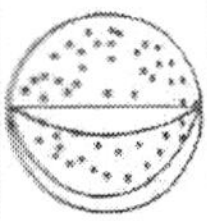		A solid screen strip parallel to wall cuts out the lower rays of the sun.

Example of Various Types of Shading Devices in Horizontal Type
Diagram 9

23

Significance of Applied Color Tilak & Bindi

Hindus apply 'Tilak/Bindi'. Men apply 'Tilak', while women apply 'Bindi' on their foreheads. It is most relevant and important to know that the sacred Tilak and Bindi are not only used by the Hindus, but its evidence has been traced in the ancient paintings and Japan. Historians trace the mark to the ancient Dravidian culture which the Aryans imbibed. Many people are curious to know the significance, meaning and secret of Tilak or Bindi and why it is applied.

There are many varieties of Tilak of Bindi having different shape and color according to beliefs and traditions of the people. These are virtually SYMBOLS and depict respect paid to Gods Brahma, Vishnu and Shiva (Mahesh).

A. The 'U' shaped Tilak/Bindi as shown in Diagram 'A' represents the 'Charan' (foot) of Lord Vishnu.

B. The half moon shaped line as shown in Diagram 'B' represents the Shiva.

C. The life stories of Lord Krishna tell of 'Gopi Chandana' the paste applied by gopikas was washed by them every day, and before applying the paste again a special invocation mantra was recited. Shri Krishna himself wore a Tilak made of Kasturi (musk). Apart from the Tilak being an auspicious and religious sign, it has magical powers if

Tilak and Bindi
(Diagrams)

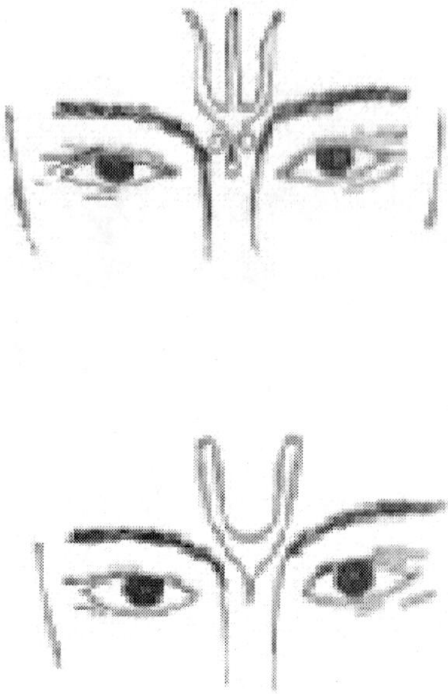

Dig - A

Dig - B

applied are significant and meaningful. For instance, a white mark is for 'people', red to gain 'control over others', yellow for material wealth and black for salvation.

The fingers used for applying the Tilak also had their own significance. The Tilak applied by the right hand thumb imparts strength, with the right hand middle finger longevity, with the ring finger sustenance and with the forefinger freedom.

The Tilak or Bindi is applied only at the centre of the forehead said to be the location of the third eye of spirituality or the eye of wisdom. In the Vedic period, People applied sandalwood paste on the forehead to cool their nervous system by way of releasing the spiritual energy within, by locating the centers of awareness.

D. The round shaped Bindi of deep red vermilion 'sindur' was and is even now applied by women on the middle of their forehead. This Bindi is considered to be auspicious and is the symbol of a married and 'Saubhagyawati' woman whose husband is alive. The Tilak or Bindi, as used today by women, is gradually changing its meaning from scientific, religious or auspicious significance to merely fashion. Ready-made Bindies are available in hundreds of varieties, colors and shapes and are face decoration rather than having much of the religious or scientific significance. Yet, there is still a feeling of auspiciousness and blessing, like 'Raksha Bandhan' and 'Bhaidooj' when the sister applies Tilak on her brother's forehead. In marriage, the bride and groom are blessed with the Tilak which is an important part of the marriage ceremony.

The following is a brief description of Tilak, different ways of its application, material used, colors, shape, and why it is applied.

Material Used	Color
• Chandan (a paste made out of Sandalwood growing in Particular forests)	Yellow, White
• Saffron (Kesar) small flower	Blood Red, Pink,
• Picked from Saffron plant	Golden Yellow
• Vibhuti (Ash) burnout ash, of Wood, charcoal, left over ash From Haven Mandal	Black, Charcoal Black and Grey
• Bindia as a part of Shrinagar made out of vegetable /flowers	All colors

As already explained in the earlier chapter that the Aryans classified themselves in four classes and divided themselves according to their duties as Brahmins, Kshtriyas, Vaishyas and Shudras, the application of Tilak, in different shape and color, was also classified according to their own classification.

Brahmins apply Tilak with their second finger round shape, white color, made from Chandan. Second finger represents Rajyogi, round shape dot represents concentration, white color represents purity and Chandan gives coolness/peace.

Kshatriyas apply Tilak with their thumb and in long shape like wick (jyoti), blood red color, made form Sindoor/Saffron. That represents strength super power/superiority.

Vaishyas apply Tilak with central tall finger round shape, golden yellow colors made from Chandan. Central finger represents prosperity, round shape stability, golden yellow color represents gold/richness, and Sandal gives cool/peace, smoothness.

Shudras apply Tilak with fourth finger, round shape, black color, mad from Vibhuti, fourth finger represents services/job, devotion, round shape represents concentration black color, represents darkness/slavery, Vibuti represents leftover ashes after the fire services.

On some special occasions, Kshatriyas and Vaishyas, after applying Tilak, put a few grains of rice which represents prosperity.

The tiny red spot upon the forehead is a mystic symbol and whatever form it takes today or will take in future, its spiritual significance in the cultural heritage cannot be forgotten.

Conclusion

Advice to Architects, Vastu Consultants, Interior Designers, Engineers, Builders & Contractors

A theory which claims to be scientific cannot claim to be final. Theories that exist have to be tested and modified, elaborated or refuted. For the reasons given previously, it is unlikely that practitioners will, of their own initiative, undertake the testing of any theory. A new field of practice research is emerging.

Further development of method requires collaboration between practitioners and researchers on case studies. There is no method that can be used on all occasions. The appropriate methods for any given architectural task are defined by the social nature of that task.

The architects play a colossal role, not only in forming a frame around existing activities, but to ensure that the frame may create new activities. Only by means of full understanding of the role of modern architecture. **To find solution, for obtaining result, it is more important to put correct questions than to give correct answers to wrong questions.**

It is worthwhile to form a habit of reacting "yes" to a new idea. The trouble with an average person is that he does not sufficiently trust himself to deliver ideas or to create new ideas.

Architects and Architecture

The environment of Architecture increasingly includes wider segments of the total society. Not only is the situation in which the architect designs for an individual client, on a site isolated from and having little impact on other surrounding building, natural environment, ecological problem, but is also expected to have concern for the users of the building. There are possible effects of the building on society at large and even on the entire world. Both professional and social value systems have to change, so that it will no longer be considered to be, by any means, sufficient for the architect to satisfy the legal owner of the building he designs.

The project itself reflects the personality and the character of the architect. In general, an architect sees himself on the side of the client and opposed to the builder.

The goal of the architect is not only simple erection of a building, from the point of view of the client and the users. The architect must visualize in connection with some on-going activities of building, its services, maintenance problem and occupiers' comforts.

Architecture is a part of building industry. This is often asserted, but seldom seriously considered, least of all, by the architects. **Books on the building industry are, in general, written by economists and management consultants, rather than architects.**

After the Second World War, architectural practices raced fast towards modernization adopting the bureaucratic values, resulting in worldwide pollution, environmental and ecological problems.

Bridging the Two Cultures Architect & Vedic Vastu

The Western Culture is like a vast desert compared to the unlimited Vedic ocean of knowledge – India is the source, the fountain-head of this vast ancient knowledge available on the planet today.

The world is out! It is an open secret that this Vedic Vastu knowledge is the most complete and elevated instruction given to man. However, on the world scale, this open secret is still relatively unknown.

When the Vedic Vastu Culture is presented through the most modern technological advances, this sublime information will be easily understood and available for all walks of life.

This is the first major attempt in history to present this vast Vedic knowledge coupled with the latest hi-tech, multi-media systems of the West.

India must give this Vedic Vastu knowledge to the world. The 'Vedas' give a whole new look to the world of architecture, art and science, scientifically, artistically and philosophically in practically every avenue of knowledge. There will be some shocking encounter to what is accurately known in this material world as Deductive thought.

This book can be an instrument in linking the East and the West together as an ideal combination. The East has a great vision in the way of its Vastu Shastras and Vedic understanding, but it is lacking materially. The West has the abundant 'resources' and advance technology, but little spiritual vision. The harmony in this combination of East-West brings a perfect whole, and a new revolution will evolve in the field of Modern Architecture and Art of Living.

'Religion Begins Where Science Ends'

Prof. Dr. B.B. Puri
Author

for further any detail please contact:

Email:- dr.bbpuri@yahoo.com
Mob:- 9999966351, 9810614201
Address:- W-151, Greater Kailash-1
New Delhi-110048, India

Some of the famous books written by Prof. Dr. B.B. Puri

- Vastu Science for 21 Century to enjoy the gift of Nature
- Applied Vastu Shastra in Modern Architecture
- Mass Scale Housing for Hot Climate
- Vedic Architecture and Art of Living
- Sick Building Syndrome & Solutions from Vastu Science
- The Art of Blissful Living. (Spiritual Laws of Vedic Philosophy)
- In Search of God: One Soul Many God
- Ageless Mind
- Life Before Death
- Natural Domestic Remedies For A Healthy Long Life
- Discover your Inner Power (Under Print)

The first edition of this book titled Vedic Architecuture and Art of Living written by the same Author Prof. B.B. Puri has been released by honourable president of India, Shri Shankar Dayal Sharma, on 26 the Dec. 1995 at Rashtrapati Bhawan, New Delhi

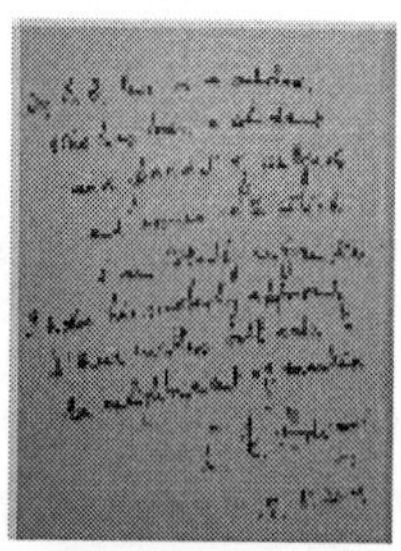

Prof. Puri is presenting his latest book "In Search of God" to Shri L.K Adwani Ji on 17th Nov 2014

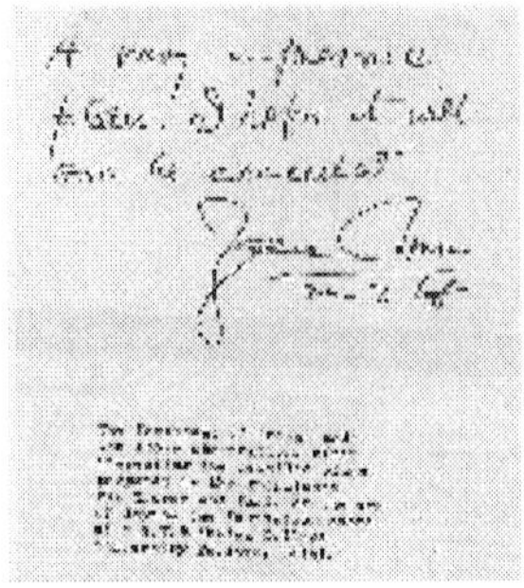

Dr. Zakir Husain, President of India Appreciating The Architecture plan of Khalsa college University of Delhi Design by Dr. B.B Puri on 24th July 1968

Prof. Puri with Smt. Indira Gandhi, Prime Minister of India receiving a Shield and Testimonial on 23rd march 1973

Prof.Puri Introducing his publisher Storyizad Moscow, to Shri. Rajiv Gandhi, Former Prime Minister of India

Dr. Puri receiving blessing from Dr. Karan Singh Cabinet Minister

Master of Wisdom Award presented to Prof. Puri by his holiness Sri Sri Ravi Shankar Ji on 26 March 2008

Prof. Dr. B.B. Puri with H.E. Mr. Anirood Jagnauth President of Mauritius on 29th may 2009 at President house Mauritius

Prof. Puri Delivering Lecture at MGI Mauritius

LETTER TO READERS

My Dear Readers,

It gives me immense pleasure in presenting to you my latest book titled "ADD COLORS IN YOUR LIFE – THROUGH VASTU SHASTRA - A SCIENCE OF VEDIC ARCHITECTURE.

After an overwhelming response to my earlier books on the same subject titled: Vastu Science for 21st Century – to enjoy the gift of nature, Vedic Architecture & Art of Living, Applied Vastu Shastra in Modern Architecture and Vastu Shastra for Mass Scale Housing for Hot Climate.

This book has made an excellent effort to establish the fact that Vastu Shastra is not merely an art but a definite Science in itself. I have written this book after the deep research of my 40 years of experience.

The knowledge of Vastu is based on Vedic Literature and is derived from the fundamental principles of Vedantic Knowledge.

This book helps you in creating and maintaining a proper balance between body, mind, soul, intellect and the environment around you, balancing with the five elements of Nature.

The tips given in the various chapters offers a practical way of life which satisfies your spiritual needs leading to mental peace and health along with material prosperity.

The Vastu Principles have been formulated keeping in view the cosmic influences of The Sun, the direction of Winds, the position of The Moon, the Earth's magnetic field and the influence of the entire cosmos on our planet.

May this book enlighten your intellect and environment, so that you can enjoy healthy, peaceful & comfortable living within the Laws of Nature. This book itself is a complete encyclopaedia not only for the beginners but also recommended for those who are practicing.

Prof. (Dr.) B.B. Puri
Author
CHAIRMAN
VASTU RESEARCH CENTRE (VRC)
RESEARCH INSTITUTE OF VEDIC CULTURE (NGO)

For any further enquiries please contact VRC Director Ms. Shaeyna Bansal.

www.vrcvastu.com

dr.bbpuri@yahoo.com

vrcvastu@gmail.com